COMPANIONS IN CONSPIRACY:
John Brown
&
Gerrit Smith

by
Chester G. Hearn

THOMAS PUBLICATIONS
Gettysburg PA 17325

CONTENTS

Acknowledgements

Forty years ago I became acquainted with the name John Brown when I attended Allegheny College in Meadville, Pennsylvania. A few miles from the college, Brown once lived, farmed, and operated a tannery in Randolph Township. I can still recall Skipper Knight, one of our professors, talking one evening of the mysterious John Brown. His story was so vivid that it was easy to imagine the Underground Railroad, at midnight, stretching across what became the college campus. At that time, I was not particularly interested in Brown, and if Skipper Knight is alive today, he might tell you I was not particularly interested in college, either, but that was a long time ago.

My curiosity in John Brown revived when I began studying the Civil War and writing history. After publishing several articles and four documented histories, I started to work on a novel of John Brown's life. By being an extensive researcher I compiled a huge reference library of books, articles, letters, documents, manuscripts and images of John Brown, his family, and associates. The relationship between Brown and Gerrit Smith fascinated me because their backgrounds and personalities were so dissimilar, but they shared a common interest—the abolition of slavery. This anomalous and somewhat accidental relationship had a stunning effect upon the lives of both men, one a poor tanner and the other perhaps the richest landowner in New York State.

Biographies written about Brown by Oswald Garrison Villard and Stephen B. Oates, and Gerrit Smith's biography by Ralph V. Harlow, led me to a wealth of letters and documents from Boston, Massachusetts, to Atlanta, Georgia, and Topeka, Kansas. I built a personal library of over forty references, and with the gracious help from the staff at the Massachusetts Historical Society, Boston Public Library, Kansas State Historical Society, the Boyd B. Stutler Collection in Charleston, West Virginia, Houghton Library of Harvard University, Cornell University Library, Syracuse University Library, the Villard Collection at Columbia University, and others, I located most of the source documents in existence today. I now have enough material on John Brown and Gerrit Smith to occupy the balance of my life if I had nothing better to do.

I owe a debt of gratitude to Mary Harrison and Susan Brandau at the Milton Public Library, and to Evelyn Burns at the James V. Brown Library in Williamsport,

Pennsylvania, for their kind and capable assistance in digging out old source material from libraries all over the country.

Civil War book dealers like David Zullo, Frank Reynolds, Wallace D. Pratt, Terry Murphy, Mike Owens, and others kept lengthy want lists on file and helped in the search for both primary and secondary source material long out of print.

Each year my wife, Ann, and I travel to Harpers Ferry and walk the same cobblestoned streets Brown's raiders once trod. We stand on the bridge over the Potomac and stare at the empty space once occupied by the United States Armory. We watch visitors to the Park peer into the enginehouse, now called "John Brown's Fort," and we wonder how many people realize that in 1859 the Ferry's famous Wager House then occupied roughly the same spot. And far to the north in Essex County, New York, stands John Brown's home. Like Harpers Ferry National Park, it is well maintained.

Conversely, after Gerrit Smith's great mansion in Peterboro, New York, burned to the ground, nobody thought it fitting to rebuild it as a lasting memorial to the Harpers Ferry raid. But without Gerrit Smith's influence and financial support, the raid may not have happened, and John Brown may have died penniless and in ignominy in his clapboard home on a windy hill in North Elba. Gerrit Smith deserved a share of John Brown's notoriety—perhaps a noose on the same gibbet—but Smith had money, not courage, and in a way, both men got what they deserved in different ways.

It was my wife, Ann, who gave me the idea to write this book. In returning home from one of our visits to Harpers Ferry, she said, "You really ought to write a short work on the relationship between John Brown and Gerrit Smith. It is one of history's great accidents."

COMPANIONS IN CONSPIRACY:
John Brown
&
Gerrit Smith

Introduction

J ohn Brown believed so deeply in predestination that if a leaf fell from a tree, it was God's wish. He fashioned his life after the Old Testament, interpreting its mysteries in his own way, translating them into his own acts through signs and omens, and often tormenting himself and others with his own indecision. Those of his twenty children who survived infancy lived as he lived and did as he did, sometimes mystified by their father's acts but always shackled to his demands. As Brown grew older, he became acutely aware of his failures, and thrusting them aside, he became a sleuth in search of his own destiny. He followed many trades without ever achieving a permanent measure of self-satisfaction or success. Along the bewildering road that led John Brown to Harpers Ferry, he met Gerrit Smith.

By most standards of social association, John Brown, a simple farmer and tanner from Hudson, Ohio, would not have much in common with Gerrit Smith, an enormously wealthy landowner from Peterboro (between Syracuse and Utica), New York. As a businessman, Brown stepped consistently from one disaster to another, and everyone associated with him, family and partners alike, shared in the suffering. Unlike Brown, Smith managed his land office with great skill. He made so much money that he turned to philanthropy as a means to mitigate his self-imposed guilt. He gave generously of his land and money, and through these kindly endowments attracted the notice of John Brown.

Brown probably never heard of Gerrit Smith until 1840. At the time, he was forty years of age and Smith forty-three. They shared a common cause; both men were abolitionists, they actively supported the Underground Railroad, and in the early 1840s, neither man had advocated violence as a means of solving the slave problem. Ten years later, after the Fugitive Slave Act passed, Brown, Smith, and thousands of other abolitionists became more militant and began organizing countermeasures to prevent the enforcement of the Act. Brown's radical concept of fighting slavery by an incursion into the South appealed to few wealthy abolitionists. One of them was Gerrit Smith.

In 1840, Brown learned of Smith's great patrimony indirectly when the Peterboro landowner gave Oberlin College title to thousands of acres of land in western Virginia because the institution had opened its doors to blacks. Eight years later, Smith's wealth, generosity and anti-slavery views brought John Brown, who was on the brink of another business failure, to Peterboro with a proposition that became the genesis of an enduring but strange and tangled relationship.

JOHN BROWN
(Kansas State Historical Society, Topeka)

Emotionally, the two men were distinctly different. John Brown never spoke or uttered an opinion that he had not first resolutely settled in his own mind and bolstered himself to stubbornly defend. He had no sense of humor, only a determined and self-righteous sense of justice straight out of the Old Testament. He lived during a time when the Golden Rule influenced public life. He cloaked himself in the Book of Judges, sitting as God's magistrate—condemning those who advocated slavery but justifying his own acts with Christian doctrine.

Gerrit Smith was gentle, affable, consoling, virtuous, and an outspoken reformist who struggled with his conscience over the matter of his great wealth. As a reformer, he spent years experimenting with almost every subject of popular interest, particularly slavery, temperance, religion, peace and politics. He fashioned himself as an independent thinker, and tried to test his convictions with an open mind, but he

GERRIT SMITH
(Madison County Historical Society, Oneida, NY)

was easily influenced. At times he manifested dogmatic characteristics and at others a penchant for accepting new premises without careful scrutiny. He changed his mind frequently, but because of his great wealth he could think as he wished. He always attracted support, and people who attached themselves to his many causes did so because Smith financed them. Different reform groups, especially the abolitionists, engaged him to give keynote addresses knowing that through patronization Mr. Smith would contribute handsomely to their organizations. Underneath the façadé of independence was a mind that could be persuaded, twisted to the right or left, and excited by glorious causes.

The Kansas-Nebraska Act of 1854 linked Brown and Smith together, and the chain of events that followed bonded the two men in an act of conspiracy and treason. This peculiar relationship flourished because Brown, who was poor but brave, gave Smith, who was wealthy but weak, a Christian cause to support in which he deeply believed.

Disorder and civil war in Kansas made a deep impression on the highly sensitive mind of peaceful, abolitionist Smith. To a man who seldom left his white-columned mansion in Peterboro, the violence in Kansas appeared to be another inevitable example of the criminal intentions of "slave power." After years of battling slavery by political means, Northern reformers and philanthropists felt bitter toward the government. Smith still hoped the question of slavery in the territories could be settled peacefully but he began to have doubts. He fought back first by giving moral support, but later he gave financial aid to free-soil fighters operating in Kansas. Over a span of three years, he spent thousands of dollars to aid Kansas emigrants. After this hefty outlay of cash, it was comparatively easy for Smith to condone and pledge money to almost any scheme for setting slaves free.

John Brown sensed the malleability of Smith's mind-set early in their relationship. He could weave a spell over the minds of young impressionable men, like the twenty-two lads who followed him to Harpers Ferry. He could cast the same spell over vulnerable adults like Gerrit Smith and five other influential members of the Secret Six who backed his Kansas raids and financed his Virginia enterprise. Brown, perhaps more than anyone else, converted Smith from an advocate of abolition by nonviolent means to an outspoken disunionist who preached emancipation by bloodshed.

At the age of fifty-six, Brown gave up most expectations of personal wealth and comfort and dedicated the balance of his life to the slave issue. He admittedly went to Kansas not to settle but "to see if something might not turn up to his advantage." Brown had always been a hard-working opportunist, and he had been raised to hate slavery. Whenever business fortunes turned against him, he believed the Lord had intervened to redirect him into the fight for emancipation. Some contemporaries who lived during his time referred to this fixation as monomania, but there is nothing in his letters or documents to suggest any form of insanity. Those who called him a monomaniac did not know him as did his family, friends, and supporters. Gerrit Smith knew him only as "dear John Brown," a humble, sacrificing Christian willing to give up his life to end slavery.

John Brown lived by the Old Testament, and shaped much of the last four years of his life around its ancient principles of violence. Gerrit Smith encouraged John Brown, perhaps unwittingly, with support and money. The relationship between the two men was certainly anomalous, but Brown would credit it all to predestination. On the road to conspiracy, John Brown courageously gave his life, and Gerrit Smith gave his sensibility.

1

The Road to Peterboro

J ohn Brown stared out the smudged office window of Perkins & Brown's wool warehouse in Springfield, Massachusetts, and reflected on his problems. His partner, Simon Perkins, had warned him. So had his son, John Jr., who tried to keep accounts straight and manage a workable cash flow. But in the spring of 1846, Brown had declared that New England woolen mills were cheating growers by paying low, unfair prices for quality fleece. Now, two years later, the warehouse bulged with sorted and graded wool, ready for shipment, and to Brown's way of thinking, fairly priced to precise grading standards he had established. Resolved to break a coalition of wool buyers who set their own rates, he stubbornly resisted pleas from his son and his partner to lower his price and obtain badly needed cash. He looked at his stock with furtive resolve. The banks would have to wait, his growers would have to wait, and so would his partner. John Brown had made up his mind. His self-respect depended upon being right—at least this time.[1]

Born on May 9, 1800 at West Torrington, Connecticut, John Brown by 1848 had tried many occupations and succeeded at none. A dearth of money compounded by reckless debts had stalked him with the persistence of his own gaunt shadow. When a tall stripling in 1817, he had abandoned divinity training because of a chronic eye inflammation, and he never returned to finish his studies. At school, the headmaster's youngest son, Heman Hallock, remembered John as "a tall, sedate, dignified young man" who had relinquished a prosperous tanning business "for the purpose of intellectual improvement."[2] But Owen Brown, John's father, could not afford to keep his son in school. The young man returned to Hudson, Ohio, believing that the Lord wished for him to pursue a different career—but what?[3]

Brown resented quitting the ministry. One of his principles was "never to yield a point, or abandon anything he had fixed his purpose upon."[4] This fixation, combined with a staunch belief in predestination, had dominated his behavior since adolescence. At the age of eighteen John Brown never suspected that by failing to become a minister, he had suffered his first of many disappointments. For the next forty years, one failure would be followed by another.

For the next few years, young Brown ran his father's tannery, bought a farm, and married plain, practical and pious Dianthe Lusk. He fathered three of his first seven children, naming them John Jr., Jason, and Owen.[5] Anxious to emulate his father by creating his own landholdings, he moved his family to a tract of undeveloped virgin timber in Crawford County, Pennsylvania, where he cleared the land and established his own tannery. He borrowed heavily, erected buildings, bought and sold cattle, surveyed property, and built roads through the wilderness. In his free time, he started a school, sheltered runaway slaves, and ran the local post office. Tiny Dianthe, weak from childbirth and afflicted by spells of insanity, gave birth to her seventh child on August 7, 1832, an infant son who followed his mother to the grave three days later.[6]

Creditors harassed the grieving widower, demanding interest and principal, but Brown had no money and was too sick with malarial chills to collect from those in debt to him. He blamed President Andrew Jackson's "hard money" policies in 1833 for drying up cash. His financial lifeline had always been credit and now it was gone. He begged the banks for time, promising restitution. No one wanted to ruin the young, industrious, hard-working Christian widower from Ohio, but banks wanted their money.

With two toddlers and three sons between the ages of eight and eleven, John Brown looked for a housekeeper. Charles Day, a gifted blacksmith from nearby Troy township, had lost his property by endorsing notes for his friends. Like Brown, he, too, had fallen on hard times. Susan, his eldest daughter, agreed to keep house for the Browns, and because sixteen-year-old Mary Anne had nothing better to do, she came with her sister to spin. Suddenly, the lonely widower had two women in the house.

It did not take long for him to decide that young, dark haired Mary Anne had the staying power to raise his children and give him more. One day he handed her a letter offering marriage. She was so overcome that she dared not read it. In the morning when she went to the spring for water, he pursued her and demanded an answer. She was too afraid of the stern man twice her age to say no.[7]

Mary Anne Day was a big-boned woman of few words. She gave the home stability and her husband a stoic constancy, unquestioning loyalty, and thirteen children. She had little education and left all decisions to the man almost old enough to be her father.[8] Had she been more assertive, perhaps Brown would not have plunged so precipitously into the many misfortunes that set him on the road to Harpers Ferry and put him on the doorstep of Gerrit Smith's Peterboro mansion. Before the newlyweds' first child arrived in 1834, bankruptcy threatened the young family, but Brown was busy testing his options by looking for signs and omens that might suggest a novel method for reversing impending misfortune.

While John Brown scrambled to save his tumbling net worth, abolitionism germinated across the North. William Lloyd Garrison's *Liberator* published stories promoting the education of Negroes, devoting column after column to the work of other abolitionists. The struggling tanner in northwestern Pennsylvania shared Garrison's enthusiasm. One evening he drew his family together and discussed his plans. He wanted to obtain at least one black youth, give him a "good English education, learn him what we can about the history of the world, about business...and, above all, try to teach him the fear of God."

To Brown's way of thinking, there were three ways to obtain such a person. "First," he said, "to...get some Christian slaveholder to release one to us. Second, to get a free one if no one will let us have one that is slave. Third, if that does not succeed, we have...to submit to considerable privation in order to buy one."[9] John Jr., his thirteen year old son, agreed, knowing there would be another hand to help in the tanyard. Having a greater aptitude for economics than his father, he asked that a determined effort be made to obtain one at no cost to the family.

Brown's stimulus to establish a school for blacks resulted from a recent Pennsylvania law that allowed the inhabitants of a township to raise a school fund through taxation. In the early days of the settlement, Brown used the great log house by the tanyard as a school for his children and for those of his neighbors. The community, however, expressed no interest in taxing themselves to finance Brown's school, and no "Christian slaveholder" stepped forward to donate his chattel for the tanner's experiment. With no fresh capital from public taxes or any other source, Brown ran out of cash to operate his tannery, and he found it impossible to sell anything for coin or to collect old debts. With a loan from Zenas Kent, a wealthy businessman in Franklin Mills (now Kent, Ohio), he loaded his pregnant wife and six children on two wagons and in May, 1835, returned to Ohio's Western Reserve.[10]

As the family rumbled over muddy, rutted roads to Franklin Mills, Brown blamed his failures on the evils of credit and the national monetary policy. It was not his nature to ascribe blame to himself. God's hand was upon Brown, guiding him back to Ohio, commanding his destiny. After all, when financial disaster swept away ten years work in Crawford County, Pennsylvania, Zenas Kent had sent money and proposed a junior partnership in a new, large, well equipped tannery. Perhaps it was not ten years wasted but a stepping stone to greater opportunity in the booming Western Reserve. The thirty-five year old tanner could not wait to feel the intoxication of success.

He crowded his large family into a small rented cabin outside Franklin Mills, and with John Jr. and Jason he built Kent's tannery. All summer they worked, but as each day passed, Brown became increasingly annoyed at Kent, an elderly gentleman who knew nothing of vats and hides but left the impression that his money had somehow endowed him with a knowledge of tanning. Brown considered these intrusions unendurable. He ignored Kent, treated him imperiously, and blamed every delay upon his partner's lethargy. "Mr. Kent's movements are very slow," he wrote, "and I cannot alter his gait. We have had a quantity of stock [hides]...on hand since May last, considerable of which might have been tanned if Mr. Kent got the tannery in readiness as he agreed." Kent, who paid John Brown to build and operate the tannery, silently grumbled that his junior partner wasted time and money by meticulously dallying over unimportant construction details.[11]

While the rift between the two partners widened, John Brown and his boys dug foundations, cut and shaped timber, and set beams. They listened to stories drift through the countryside of speculators getting rich by buying up cheap land along the route of the proposed Pennsylvania-Ohio canal. Rumors buzzed that simple pasture land, available for $20.00 an acre, had jumped in value to $1,000.00 a few days later. This was a far easier way of making money than wielding a pick, and the junior partner suffered a pang of envy. Under his sweaty brow kindled a spark of interest. Everywhere he went, people related breathless stories of incredible riches gained by a few leading citizens with inside information, men like wise old Zenas Kent and a few of his cronies. Twenty men had formed the Franklin Land Company and began buying cheap land, all on credit. Soon, there would be no more bargains.

For a while, Brown stuck with the tannery, ignoring with equal firmness opportunity, temptation, and Zenas Kent. After his experiences in Pennsylvania, nobody surpassed the middle-aged family man in stretching his meager income and saving every penny. He still had debts, and he knew tanning was where he belonged, but his strained relationship with Kent, combined with his great need for money, weakened his resolve to stay the course. With winter coming, local farmers were obtaining short-term contracts to dig the canal. To John Brown it looked easy; all that was needed was a yoke of oxen and a plow to scoop mud and earth from a ditch thirty feet wide and four feet deep.

In November Brown decided to break with Kent and obtain a contract on a section of the canal between Franklin and Akron. In a discussion to dissolve the partnership, old Zenas Kent was so euphoric about Brown's departure that he loaned the ex-tanner all the money he needed to buy a team of oxen and a set of earth-moving implements. Soon Brown and his boys were sloshing through the winter mud, slipping and sliding as the sluggish oxen twisted about in the yoke. They paid little attention to the high-hatted dandies dressed in snug woolens who rode by in fancy coaches to smile and wave at the shivering, dirt-splattered workers in the cut.[12]

After a few weeks of wrestling with a team of stubborn oxen in snow and rain, Brown learned that Zenas Kent had pocketed $75,000.00 when he sold the Franklin Land Company's rights to water power and industrial sites on the Cuyahoga River, which ran parallel to the projected path of the canal. Everybody believed that with increased water power coming to Franklin, combined with cheap canal transportation, villages along the river would attract capital and enjoy explosive growth. Smitten by new prospects, Brown prowled the countryside with the eye of a trained surveyor and began laying out imaginary streets and plots for the future cities along the Cuyahoga. By now he had become as infected as any other speculator who rooted through idle acres looking for a quick bargain before prices rose.

Unlike Pennsylvania, wildcat banks had sprung up all over the Western Reserve and flooded the economy with bank notes backed by little specie. Credit was easy and everyone seemed to be captivated by the prospect of manifest destiny and permanent prosperity.[13] For John Brown, the temptation to turn a quick profit passed from a tantalizing whim to a frantic impulse to reap his fortune before big Eastern money grabbed up all the land. With money plentiful and inflation spreading across the country, there was no end in sight. For once in his life, Brown could borrow dollars today and pay them back tomorrow with inflated currency.

In December 1835 Brown wandered through the fields of Frederick Haymaker's ninety five acre farm on the outskirts of Franklin Mills. Looking casually about the farm, he could see the banks of the Cuyahoga to the north and west, the canal behind him, and imagine the future metropolis of Franklin rising from a clearing to the west. To a man who believed in signs and omens, something greater than his own curiosity had guided him to the Haymaker farm. Here, next to the site of the new town of Franklin, land grabbers had passed oblivious to opportunity. Brown envisioned the

Haymaker farm as strategically located to capture the overflow when the future city of Franklin began its outward expansion. Within a few months the land could be worth $1,000.00 an acre, maybe more, and Brown knew he must buy it. He borrowed from the bank, bought the farm for $7,000.00, and entered into a career of land speculation that more experienced financiers would have considered irresponsibly brazen.[14]

Brown subdivided half of the Haymaker farm, selling half-acre lots that had cost him $37.00 for $200.00, and large corner lots for $900.00. To an old friend and former partner, Seth Thompson, he offered to sell the undivided half of the farm for its original price, $7,000.00. Thompson gave Brown $1,134.00 in cash, $1,866.00 in a note due five days later, and the balance in four promissory notes payable annually until January, 1840. Instead of liquidating debt on the Haymaker property, Brown took part of the cash and made a down payment on a large parcel of land next to the farm. With other proceeds, he bought a farm with a nice farmhouse three miles from the village of Hudson and moved his family back to the area where he had lived as a child.[15]

At the age of thirty-six, the tanner turned canal digger had suddenly transformed his life into one envied by his peers. Associates with money lined up behind his projects to offer credit at usurious rates. Folks patted him on the back for grabbing the Haymaker farm out from under the Franklin Land Company. When they heard that the tall, sedate promoter-planner was looking at a parcel at Cuyahoga Falls, also on the canal, they were eager to induce a man of John Brown's stature to invest in their little community. They made him a director of the local bank and elected him to the Cuyahoga Falls Real Estate Association.[16] When he wanted to purchase the coveted Westlands property near Hudson, six friends guaranteed his $6,000.00 loan from the Western Reserve Bank of Warren. Westlands' rich cultivated fields with its rolling woodlands and gentle stream made an enviable setting for a wealthy landowner. When he drove his considerable family to the Franklin Congregational Church each Sunday, people stared at the slim, erect gentleman in the sparkling new brown broadcloth suit and a high beaver hat, and said, "There's John Brown. A few months ago he had nothing."

Developer Brown had reasons for being optimistic. Not far from the Haymaker lots, Edmund Munroe, a Boston millionaire, had collected subscriptions of more than $500,000.00 to establish the Munroe Falls Manufacturing Company, an expansive silk company in the heart of the Western Reserve. Farmers began buying more land, planting mulberry trees, and importing silk worms to feed on the leaves and spin their cocoons. Land values soared to new heights. Hedging his good luck, Brown carved a road through the Haymaker tract and called it Munroe Street.[17]

At least one local merchant doubted Brown's business sagacity. Marvin Kent, son of old Zenas, had taken over the tannery and eventually became even wealthier than his father. He knew Brown and considered him constitutionally incapable of taking advice. "Brown saw everything large," Kent said, "and felt himself the equal of anything. He had such fast, stubborn and strenuous convictions that nothing short of mental rebirth could ever have altered." Years after the Civil War he declared that Brown had no interest in slavery, only in making money.[18]

The new landowner's emphasis may have shifted to making money, but his abolitionist views had not changed. One Sunday, during an interdenominational revival gathering at the Franklin Congregational Church, he noticed that a group of blacks had been herded to the back. He stopped the preacher in the midst of his sermon and chastised him for segregating colored members of the congregation. The reverend, stunned by the interruption, stood silent, and all heads turned to the tall grim man with the challenging metallic voice. Defiantly, John Brown led his family to the rear of the church and beckoned the blacks forward, seating them in his pew. A day later several deacons visited Brown at his home and labored in vain to explain to him the error of his ways. He glared at them frostily and refused to kneel and join them in prayer. They departed, scolded and rebuked.[19]

In mid-1836 the federal government initiated another monetary panic by refusing to accept promissory notes, mortgages, state bank scrip, and other so-called securities exchanged for purchases of land. Brown's backers grew uneasy. They had not received a return on their investments, not even a joint deed for their share of Brown's purchases. Seth Thompson, with $7,000.00 committed to Brown's enterprises, wanted out. Brown replied, "Try and trust all with a wise & gracious God."[20] Thompson asked his partner to dispose of the property before the economy collapsed. Six months later Brown was still beseeching Thompson to have patience. "I do think it is best to sell out if we can come at anything like a fair rate, but I think the time unfavorable. If we have been crazy in getting in, do try & lets exercise a sound mind about the manner of getting out."[21]

As long as the Cuyahoga flowed and work on the canal continued, John Brown was willing to stave off his creditors and wait for better days. When work stopped on the canal, lots that sold for $1,000.00 dropped to less than $100.00 or were auctioned off to pay back taxes. Brown's creditors would wait no longer. Eleven of Akron's fourteen merchants failed, and some were sent to jail. Brown could not face the indignity of a cell, but still he held out. Old friends deserted him, squared their accounts with the banks, and engaged lawyers to obtain title to their collateral. Acre by acre, farm by farm, John Brown's fortunes collapsed in a dismal thud upon the heads of his considerable family.[22]

Legal suits began piling up against Brown's promissory notes, and when the Western Reserve Bank tried unsuccessfully to collect on a $6,000.00 note, they levied judgments on Brown's six endorsers. Only one, Heman Oviatt, had enough attachable assets to be vulnerable. Brown agreed to surrender the Westlands farm to Oviatt in exchange for liquidating the debt. Oviatt paid off the note, but the bank issued the deed in Brown's name. Brown failed to notify Oviatt. Next, to pay off other debts, he remortgaged Westlands to two new investors. In another transaction, Daniel C. Gaylord obtained a judgment against Brown and forced the sale of Westlands by the sheriff. Amos Chamberlain, another of Brown's friends, bought the farm with the idea that Brown would eventually have the money to buy it back. Oviatt had paid off Brown's bank loan in exchange for Westlands but Chamberlain now held title to the farm.

Brown refused to surrender the use of Westlands to Chamberlain or Oviatt, insisting that he still had the right to pasture his cattle there. With John Jr., Jason, and Owen, he boarded up a small log cabin and with old fashioned muskets guarded the property day and night. Chamberlain owned the property, but every time he attempted to reason with his old friend, Brown waved a musket in his face and ordered him away. Finally Chamberlain lost patience, filed a warrant, and the sheriff of Portland County rode out to the farm with a posse and arrested Brown and his boys. After a few days in the Akron jail, Brown wrote an apologetic letter to Chamberlain, explaining the "misunderstanding." Eventually, Chamberlain burned down the shanty of momentary rebellion and dropped all charges against Brown. With head down, the sullen speculator, confused by conveyances, mortgages, deeds and lawsuits, gathered his sons and ignominiously headed home.[23]

In an effort to make ends meet and seek relief from his burdensome debts, Brown began driving Seth Thompson's cattle across Pennsylvania to Connecticut. There he discovered a flourishing knitting industry with mills in every town. The towns and cities bustled with manufacturing energy. Agents told him the future was in wool, not hides and meat, or for that matter, silk. American mills could not buy enough fleece from domestic growers and resented paying higher prices for English wools. A man who sought guidance from signs and omens, Brown became smitten by a boyhood dream, to become a keeper of sheep and walk through green pastures. Disregarding the need to economize, he dipped into his leather pouch of borrowed money and purchased ten full-blooded Saxony sheep.[24]

Seth Thompson and Heman Oviatt must have been satisfied with the proceeds from the first cattle drive because they sent John Brown and his boys east with another herd. On this trip the aspiring shepherd traveled to Boston to obtain a loan. He returned to West Hartford with no cash, but he expected the loan to be approved and made daily visits to the post office looking for the draft. During Brown's wait, George Kellogg, agent for the New England Woolen Company in Rockville, Connecticut, handed Brown $2,800.00 to be used to buy Ohio wool for the firm. Expecting the imminent arrival of his loan, Brown used Kellogg's money to cover his debts. He was shocked when word came that his loan had been denied. He explained to Kellogg how he had misused the woolen company's funds, signing the letter "Unworthily yours." Already insolvent, Brown nonetheless pledged to make up the loss, and Kellogg could not bring himself to prosecute so honest and so penitent a thief.[25]

Late in 1839 the federal court assigned Judge George DePeyster the task of unraveling and liquidating John Brown's holdings for the benefit of his creditors. Even the abundant power of the Cuyahoga River, upon which Brown had depended for financial salvation, had been diverted by the canal company to provide more water to property owned by its directors. The Haymaker farm, Brown & Thompson's addition, and all the land around Franklin plummeted back to $20.00 an acre.

As the process of bankruptcy gradually impoverished the family, Brown looked for alternatives. His father, who had astutely avoided investing in his son's schemes, was a trustee at Oberlin College. The elder Brown remembered that Gerrit Smith, a wealthy landowner from Peterboro, New York, had endowed the college with an enormous tract of land in western Virginia (now in Doddridge and Tyler Counties, West Virginia). Plagued by title disputes, the Board of Trustees hired John Brown to survey the land, paid him a dollar a day plus expenses, provided him with an outfit, and offered him the opportunity to buy one thousand acres at a nominal sum with adequate time to pay. Undoubtedly, John Brown learned from his father that Smith's generous gift to Oberlin was to reward the college for opening its doors to black students. The penniless tanner would not forget the name Gerrit Smith or the wealthy landowner's generous patrimony.[26]

In April, 1840, Brown packed his surveying instruments and with his sons headed into the wilderness of western Virginia. Three months later he was back in Hudson refreshed and invigorated. The Board of Trustees read his report and on August 28 offered to "convey by deed to Brother John Brown...one thousand acres of our western Virginia land."[27]

During his jaunt to Virginia, more claims against his assets had been filed and waited in abeyance for his return. He still owed Heman Oviatt $5,668.00, and Oviatt, had he wanted, could have charged Brown with fraud. Oviatt suggested ways that Brown could honor the debt. As a consequence, four months passed before Brown responded to Oberlin's generous land offer. Partly because of Brown's procrastination, the board had experienced a change of heart. They decided to retain the land and perhaps sell it later to bolster their own balance sheet. The decision came as a blow to Brown, who now had eleven children.[28] Oviatt was pleased to learn that Brown would not be running off to another state. He now envisaged a way to recover his lost capital by engaging the insolvent speculator and his considerable family in two enterprises: first, the care of his large flock of sheep, and second, a tannery. Brown agreed to manage both as a junior partner until the debt was paid.[29] In the meantime, Judge DePeyster sold Brown's farmhouse at public auction and forced the family to move into a small cabin on Oviatt's sheep farm in Richfield. Finally, on September 28, 1842, Brown availed himself of a new federal bankruptcy law, officially declared bankruptcy under its provisions, surrendered all his assets, and was legally cleared of any obligation to pay his outstanding debts, including the one owed to Oviatt. The court stripped the Browns of every possession but clothing and "other articles and necessities."[30] Jason Brown, who was then about eighteen, later described those days by saying, "Oh, we were poor!"[31]

Brown overcame the embarrassment of bankruptcy and soon established himself as a remarkable shepherd, but a deadly pestilence lurked in the nearby spring where the family drew its drinking water. In September, 1843, Charles, age five, fell ill, followed by Sarah, nine, Peter, two, and the infant Austin. The tired shepherd sat up night after night, slowly watching his children slip away, wondering if his were the sins calling up God's rebuke. As each child died, he felt powerless to stem the flow of predestination. To the father, it was hard to accept the Lord's judgment when it punished the guilty by striking down the innocent. But in John Brown's world, not a drop of rain fell from the heavens without a reason, and he groped introspectively to understand the meaning of God's harsh message.[32]

After two and a half years of working off his debt to Heman Oviatt, Brown was approached by Colonel Simon Perkins, one of the wealthiest men in the Western Reserve. Perkins offered him a junior partnership to manage the colonel's large herd of Saxony sheep. Brown accepted, and on April 10, 1844, moved his family to Mutton Hill, outside Akron, and into a spacious cottage overlooking the rolling countryside.[33]

Perkins, a small, docile man with a goatee, owed his wealth to his father, a founder of Akron, but the colonel was almost as deficient in business acumen as Brown. The junior partner took hold of the herd as if it were his own and tacitly disregarded suggestions from the owner. Perkins obediently stepped aside and admitted, "I had no controversy with John Brown for it would have done no good." Perhaps there was justification for Perkins' passive submission. The editor of the *Ohio Cultivator* wrote, "Too much cannot be said in praise of these sheep, and especially in the care and skill displayed by Mr. Brown."[34]

Brown traveled frequently between Ohio, western Virginia, and New England, attending fairs and collecting praise for his fine Saxony stock. He talked with wool growers, who all complained of being exploited by Eastern buyers who paid less for their fleece than it was worth. Brown suggested establishing a warehouse in the East where wool could be graded, stored, and sold at fair prices. The program described by Brown would operate as a cooperative, and everybody would share in the benefits derived from uniform grading standards and fair pricing. Perkins, who had not learned to ask Brown basic, fundamental business questions, agreed to finance the venture. Growers, who knew Brown only as a competent herdsman, agreed to send all their fleece to his novel cooperative. With John Jr. as his accountant and Jason as his grader, Brown leased a warehouse in Springfield, Massachusetts, and set up shop. Most of the younger boys remained on Mutton Hill and managed Perkins & Brown's fine flock. In no time at all, John Brown was up to his neck in fleece.[35]

Unfortunately, Brown was no more adept at negotiating prices with woolen mills, or keeping accounts straight, than he was in managing money or land titles. He ignored market prices, the price mills would be willing to pay for his graded fleece, and set his own rates. As a consequence, wool moved slowly and the warehouse became stacked to the ceiling, forcing Perkins & Brown into a much larger warehouse.

For most of 1846 and part of 1847, Brown seemed content with progress. Wool continued to flow into the warehouse— not out. He considered his burgeoning inventories an asset and assured doubtful growers that buyers would soon be converging on the warehouse with open purses. Back in Ohio, Simon Perkins grew restless as unpaid bills stacked up on his Akron desk. Growers needed money and pleaded with Brown to sell their stocks. A few lots sold from inventory created more confusion. Fleece became commingled and John Jr. could not determine who to pay. Perkins received a torrent of more angry letters. He admitted having no control over the situation but promised to investigate the problems. Independently, Brown satisfied some growers and a few irate creditors by borrowing from the bank, a little now, a little more later. Brown was a good juggler— he had done it all before.[36]

Perkins & Brown was already headed for disaster when in December, 1846, an Englishman stopped by the warehouse and bought for export a huge lot of fine fleece. Unfortunately, the unexpected purchase convinced Brown that his strategy had been right.[37] In 1847, he processed 500,000 pounds of fleece, temporized in fixing his price, annoyed potential buyers with his deliberations, and ended the year with more inventory. To make more room, he reduced the price on inferior wool twenty-five percent below market. Aaron Erickson, a veteran New York wool dealer, cautioned Brown that manufacturers would buy up the discounted grades immediately. Brown snapped back, "Let them take them...I will make it up on my fine wool," which he had graded fifty percent above market. Erickson bowed out of the warehouse convinced that Brown was "a victim of his own delusions."[38]

As problems in the wool business multiplied, Brown received disturbing news from Mary. Seventeen year old Ruth had accidently scalded Amelia, Mary's ninth child, and the baby soon died. Because of business problems, he could not go to Akron, but like every other turn in his life, he ascribed it to God's eternal meddling. To some degree he blamed himself, writing,

> If I had a right sence of my habitual neglect of my familys Eternal interests; I should probably go crazy. I humbly hope this dreadful afflictive Providence will lead us all more properly to appreciate the amazeing, unforeseen, untold, consequences; that hang upon the right or wrong doing of things seemingly of trifling account. Who can tell or comprehend the vast results for good, or for evil; that are to follow the saying of one little word.[39]

The accident convinced Brown that his young family must be brought to Springfield. The boys could look after the Perkins & Brown flock on Mutton Hill without their mother. Nonetheless, Akron neighbors wondered why the absent shepherd could not find more time to spend with his family.

If the loss of Amelia failed to dampen the unshakable determination of the wool merchant, Congress delivered an unexpected blow by reducing the tariffs on imported wool. High-grade Saxony fleece dropped from 75 cents to 25 cents a pound. The Mexican War, which started on May 13, 1846, destabilized the wool market, and for a while prices ebbed and flowed with no certain direction. Brown, unable to adjust his thinking or his prices to external factors, tenaciously insisted that buyers would ultimately pay his price. While he waited for that day to come, he paced the streets of Springfield and immersed himself in anti-slavery activities.[40]

After settling his family in a small house on Franklin Street, just around the corner from Perkins & Brown, he met Frederick Douglass, Henry Highland Garnet, and James W. Loguen, all black ministers who listened intently to the slim, gaunt businessman talk of attacking slavery. As he metered out hints of his plan in a measured metallic voice, they watched the fire in his grey-blue eyes and began to believe that this white man was unlike other abolitionists. His was not idle talk, but they wondered if he understood his own proposals. Eventually, all of them would help Brown raise money, but with frail resolve.

Brown recognized that among his black friends no one commanded more respect or possessed more influence than Frederick Douglass, a tall, handsome, six foot mulatto who had been born into slavery in 1817. He had escaped north at the age of nineteen, joined the Massachusetts Anti-Slavery Society as a lecturer in 1841, and in Rochester, New York, eventually founded the *North Star*, an abolitionist newspaper that favored legal and political methods for ending slavery. Brown invited him to his home to discuss "urgent matters." Douglass was on a lecture tour, but both Loguen and Garnet strongly recommended that he meet with that "lean, impressive" white man. Finally in November, 1847, Douglass tapped on the door of Perkins & Brown and then trailed the fast-gaited wool merchant to his sparsely furnished home for a plain, simple meal.[41]

After Mary cleared away the supper dishes, Brown unfolded a large map and spread it upon the table. "These mountains," he said, running his thin, bony finger along the Alleghenies, "are the basis of my plan. God has given the strength of the hills to freedom; they were placed here for emancipation of the negro race; they are full of natural forts, where one man for defense will be equal to a hundred for attack; they are full of good hiding places, where large numbers of brave men could be concealed, baffle and elude pursuit for a long time." Brown explained that he would destroy the value of slave property by rendering it insecure. He was "not averse to the shedding of blood." The use of guns would give black men "a sense of their manhood...No people could have self respect, or be respected, who would not fight for their freedom."

Douglass saw many flaws in the plan but was struck by Brown's intensity and great confidence that the plan would work. The ex-slave did not advocate violence. In fact he feared it, but here was a white man whose "own soul had been pierced with the iron of slavery." Perhaps, just perhaps, this strong, sinewy, forty-seven year old self-styled abolitionist had put his finger on a truism, that "slavery could only be destroyed by bloodshed."[42]

"But they would employ bloodhounds to hunt you out of the mountains," Douglass warned.

"That they might attempt," Brown replied, "but the chances are, we should whip them, and when we...whipt one squad, they would be more careful how they pursued."

"But you might be surrounded and cut off from your provisions..."

"We would cut our way out," Brown said, adding that even if the worst came, he could but be killed, and he had no better use for his life than to lay it down for the cause of the slave.[43]

The two men talked long into the night. When Douglass left Brown's home in the morning, he was half convinced that only force and blood would liberate the four million souls living in bondage. Douglass had not seen the last of John Brown.

In the spring of 1848, John Brown stared gloomily at rack after rack of unsold wool and commiserated over a stack of unpaid bills. Jason had returned to Ohio, disgusted with the business, and married Ellen Sherbondy. Seventeen year old Frederick was suffering from a mental affliction diagnosed as "an accumulation of blood on the brain." Twenty-six year old John Jr. married an Ohio girl, Wealthy Hotchkiss, but because he hoped to prevent his father from enduring another bankruptcy he brought his bride to Springfield to clerk for Perkins & Brown. Mary was pregnant again and due any day. Growers left their farms, traveled to Springfield, and begged for money. Simon Perkins sent directives from Akron, but the junior partner set them aside with the unpaid bills.

For John Brown, it was time for a change. Misfortune stalked him like a curse. Already creditors threatened lawsuits and once-friendly bankers manifested signs of surliness. He could not endure another bankruptcy. If God had intended him to succeed in the wool business, He would not have led him to the verge of failure. Perhaps his mission was not to succeed in business. Perhaps his was something else, something more noble, but whatever it was, Perkins & Brown was nearing its end. There would be no reason to keep his family in Springfield, and no financial basis for supporting them there.

As he stared out the smudged windows of the warehouse, he remembered western Virginia and one thousand acres of rich land which had slipped through his fingers, land donated by a man named Gerrit Smith. He had learned that Smith, in a gesture of great patrimony, had recently set aside 120,000 acres of land in the Adirondack Mountains for negro families who wanted to farm and become respected citizens. But in the mountains winters were long and cold, and the tired wool merchant wondered if displaced blacks could survive in the harsh north country. They might need help. And John Brown, who needed help himself, decided to pay generous Mr. Smith a visit.[44]

2
A Truly Noble Cause

O n April 8, 1848, a slim gentleman in a dark deacon-like suit knocked on the
door of Gerrit Smith's white-columned Peterboro mansion. Smith did not
recognize the stranger, but he had become accustomed to all sorts of unexpected
visitors appearing on his doorstep, some black and some white—all desperate and
seeking aid from the generous philanthropist. He offered them food, clothing, and a
little money. To those who came to him sick, he provided care in one of the many
rooms of his spacious three-floor home. Blacks, both free and slave, some fleeing
from bounty hunters up from the South, filtered through Peterboro to apply for one
of the three thousand farms Smith had set aside in eight counties of New York State.
The rocky land in the Adirondacks, Essex County, was scrubbed and difficult to
cultivate. But Smith believed that there blacks could improve their material condition, giving up "notions of being servants and become independent mechanics and
farmers." By farming their land, they would earn self-respect and avoid those who
hated them. But when Smith invited John Brown into his luxurious parlor, he could
not have guessed how the intense, modest wool merchant would affect the balance
of his life.[1]

Brown had a proposition and got right to the point. "Mr. Smith," he said, "I am
something of a pioneer; I grew up among the woods and wild Indians of Ohio, and
am used to the climate and ways of life that your negro colony find so trying. I will
take one of your farms myself, clear it up and plant it, and show my colored neighbors
how such work should be done; will give them work as I have occasion, look after
them in needful ways, and be a kind of father to them."[2]

Smith, a six-foot, 200-pound somewhat fleshy man, was impressed by Brown's
hard muscularity, his slim 150-pound youthful body, and the self-reliance and personal
determination it implied. Brown stood as he talked, giving the appearance of a man
much taller than his five-feet-eleven-inch frame. He spoke knowledgeably of farming, of his life-long interest in the abolition of slavery, and of his adherence to
Scripture-based principles. Brown mentioned nothing of his ventures in land specu-

GERRIT SMITH'S MANSION
(Madison County Historical Society, Oneida, NY)

lation or the wool business. Smith was delighted to help a man with Brown's good credentials. Having a man of Brown's stature and good intentions available would relieve his worry over the blacks who had settled in Essex County. In time, it would relieve him of much more.[3]

When Brown left Peterboro, he had options on two farms, subject to his inspection and acceptance. He also asked for options on farms for his sons. When Smith seemed hesitant, Brown deferred the request until the new relationship became cemented in friendship.

Brown had sharp instincts for sizing up people, and he detected much about Gerrit Smith's underlying personality during the lengthy discussion in his new benefactor's parlor. Brown found Smith a little naive, a somewhat open and pleasant country gentleman who could afford to subsidize his own opinions.

Smith's strong abolitionist convictions differed from Brown's. Smith supported the Liberty Party, a small group of activists who believed that slavery could be snuffed out through the political process. Brown stood for violence, but he did not press the issue with his customary fervor. Had he done so, he would have discovered that Smith's convictions could sometimes be altered by discreet persuasion. Under that enormous wealth was an eccentric individual driven by impulse, stormy at times and almost childlike at others, but always a cheerful and charming host. Smith spent money for any cause he thought was right, and believed that God watched his outpourings of cash with divine approval or disapproval, which explains why Smith suffered unshakable hypochondria and visions of impending death. Through all his doubts and haunting fears, Smith remained a dedicated philanthropist, partially because of his great wealth and partially because of his early religious views.[4]

Born March 6, 1797, in Utica, New York, to Peter and Elizabeth Livingston Smith, young Gerrit had the advantage of growing up with a father who, after a lucrative three year partnership with John Jacob Astor, became a successful land speculator. When Gerrit was nine, the Smiths moved to Peterboro. The young lad obtained his education in local schools, the family church, and from long hours of hard work on the immense family farm. Throughout Gerrit's youth, his father continued to acquire huge tracts of land in Madison, Oneida, Oswego and Onondaga counties.

At seventeen, Gerrit Smith enrolled at Hamilton College in Clinton, New York, a short ride by horseback from Peterboro. After a few months of adjustment, he developed into an excellent student. Smith graduated in 1818, and the following year married Wealtha Ann Backus, the daughter of the college president. With guidance from his father, Smith wasted no time in launching a career in real estate. At the age of twenty-two, and operating on a scale that would have stunned John Brown, he purchased 18,000 acres of land near Florence, New York. In his first big plunge, Smith exceeded the limits of his available credit and barely escaped bankruptcy, but unlike Brown, he made it work. About the same time, his bride of seven months suddenly died.[5]

Peter Smith, who was beginning to experience difficulty keeping track of his own vast holdings, decided it was time to turn the family business over to his son. In 1820, young Smith and Daniel Cady, Gerrit's uncle, began to share responsibility for nearly a million acres of land. The task exposed Gerrit to great power and wealth, but with it came a throbbing guilt that one man should not have so much when so many others lived in need. Wealth also exposed him to the same horrendous fluctuations of the national economy that led to Brown's financial ruin in Pennsylvania and his bankruptcy in Ohio. Smith, too, for all his land and money, barely remained solvent during the panic of 1837. Financial worries frayed his nerves and made him ill. For seven years he fought disaster. Helped by a timely loan from John Jacob Astor, he weathered the long depression, and when the economy improved in the mid-1840s, his financial affairs stabilized and once again money began to flow.

At the age of twenty-five Smith remarried, this time to Ann Carol Fitzhugh, a sensible young woman with good business instincts. Since the land office operated out of their home, she insisted upon understanding ledgers and accounts. Four children could not keep her separated from her husband's land speculations, and during the grim years following the panic of 1837 when Smith could not afford clerks, his wife and daughter helped to manage the accounts and conserve the cash. Unlike John Brown's family, the Smiths always managed to live well, and Gerrit, the perennial hypochondriac, patiently encouraged his wife to participate in the business.

After Smith remarried, he continued his lifelong study of religion, and when two of his children died, he accepted their deaths in the fashion of the time—predestination. For more than twenty years he studied Protestant theology and practice, giving generously to the American Tract and Bible Society and the American Sunday School Union. At the same time, he questioned the bigotry of sectarianism and debated the necessity of baptism. Condemned by members of the ministry for preaching politics on Sunday, Smith countered their criticism and in 1843 built and became the minister of his own church in Peterboro. He extended membership to all "true Christians" who lived in Peterboro whether or not they attended services. Two years later, after further religious study, he announced that Saturday, not Sunday, was the real Sabbath.[6]

During the same period of time, John Brown, who had been steeped since childhood in Calvinistic theology, withdrew from the Congregationalist church and became what his son, John Jr., described as an independent Christian Socialist. Brown was too independent, however, to ever allow anyone to stigmatize his beliefs by giving them a name. John Jr. said that "Father's favorite theme was that of the Community plan of cooperative industry, in which all should labor for the common good; having all things in common as did the disciples of Jesus in his day." Approaching the matter of religion from different directions, especially on the matter of slavery, Gerrit Smith and John Brown had much in common. Brown believed that those who worked the land should own it, and Smith believed in providing land to those willing to work it. At the close of his life, Smith remarked, "God gives me money to give away." John Brown had no money and offered his life instead.[7]

In addition to spending thousands of dollars to promote religious and moral reform, women's rights, and temperance crusades, Smith sponsored a variety of educational projects aimed at promoting black self-help. A manual labor school established in 1834 on his land in Peterboro motivated him to carve out a tract of land in Essex County and grant small farms to deserving black families. In the same year, John Brown and his brother Frederick discussed raising money through taxes to establish a school for blacks in Crawford County, Pennsylvania. Brown's plan never materialized because it required public funding. Smith's plan worked because he had thousands of acres of rock-infested and marginal land in the Adirondacks to give away and because no sensible farmer would ever settle there.[8]

After making substantial annual endowments to colleges, universities, libraries and pet humanitarian projects, Smith spent as much as $5,000.00 a year for the rescue and maintenance of fugitives from southern slavery. Brown, who kept poor accounts on whatever he did, sheltered runaway slaves from his early years in Ohio and Pennsylvania. He fed, clothed and cared for them in hidden quarters built into his barn, then secreted them through the night to the next stop on the Underground Railroad.[9] Active in the Underground Railroad while living in Springfield, Brown even tried to raise money for an African high school he hoped to establish in Canada. With respect to blacks, Brown and Smith shared similar philosophies, for both recognized that only with education would blacks achieve equality.[10]

About 1830, Smith joined the American Colonization Society because it was the first political organization calling for the emancipation of slaves. He pledged $10,000.00, which he regretted after realizing that the majority of its members wanted to banish the Negro from American society.

William Lloyd Garrison, outspoken publisher of *The Liberator*, argued against colonization. He wanted to break the chains of the black man, guarantee him protection under the law, preserve his family, give him education, and provide him with religious training. Garrison argued that the Negro had been westernized and could not survive in the jungles of Africa or some uninhabited island in the Caribbean. The whites had brought them to America and were now responsible for making them "economically secure" in white society. Garrison advocated a nonviolent crusade, one which condemned slavery because it denied God to blacks and whites alike, and which sought to resurrect the slaveholder from the ignominy of his sinful ways. Unlike many abolitionists, Garrison never turned to violence. Thirty years later, he opposed the war until after Abraham Lincoln issued the Proclamation Emancipation.[11]

In 1833 Garrison convinced scattered groups of New York abolitionists to join together to form the National Antislavery Society. Abolition in New York consisted of several factions. While Garrisonians mobilized to take the battle to Washington, D.C., the Gerrit Smith circle, centered mostly in Madison, Oneida, and Oswego Counties, quietly advocated "cultural voluntarism," a more visionary aspect of freedom designed around small communities. Smith believed that individuals should be free to do good—to build railroads, canals, schools, churches, or to engage in any activity that did not violate God's moral imperatives. Cultural voluntarism assumed that all people, black and white, deserved the same freedom to act morally. There would be no privileged class, "distinctions of rank" or "separation of individuals from the common lot." The slave system represented the grossest example of aristocracy, for it gave masters unwarranted privileges and denied bondsmen "the inherent right of self-ownership."[12]

After several years of somewhat passive involvement, Gerrit Smith and his wife attended the antislavery convention in Utica in 1835. They were on their way to visit Gerrit's father in Schenectady and stopped in Utica out of simple curiosity. No sooner had the meeting been called to order when a mob crowded inside, interrupted the proceedings with abusive yelling, and threatened violence to speakers who took the podium. Outraged by the intrusion, Smith sprang to his feet declaring that he was no abolitionist but believed in fair play. When his appeal failed to prevent the dispersion of the assembly, he invited the convention to adjourn to Peterboro where they could hold an uninterrupted meeting the next day. Instead of going on to Schenectady, he returned home, woke all the servants, and began making preparations for an indefinite number of guests. Nearly four hundred delegates turned up, beginning with about thirty for breakfast, eighty for dinner, and over a hundred for tea. Later, over forty delegates stretched out on Smith's sofas, lounges and carpets for a good night's rest. When they returned to their homes, their hearts still pounded from hearing Smith's great speech filled with thrilling resolutions. A fresh flood of enthusiasm swept the delegates off their feet, for that day Gerrit Smith became an abolitionist and pledged his financial support.[13]

Smith, suddenly at center stage in New York's antislavery movement, never stopped working for the cause into which he so precipitously hurled himself. For many years to come, he still listened to arguments for colonization, and admitted that they sometimes made sense. As time passed and polarization mounted between North and South, his advocacy of outright emancipation grew stronger. With his money and influence, he began to unify New York's antislavery factions into a cohesive political force. He coupled his donations with strong intimations that group members cease their personal squabbles and work cooperatively. He still pressed to end slavery by political means, but began to doubt if politicians would ever agree on a solution. He supported the Liberty Party in the early 1840s. When those efforts failed, he joined the Liberty League. By the mid-1840s, Smith estimated that he had contributed over $50,000.00 to the antislavery crusade, a substantial sum of money when compared to the small return.[14]

By 1848 Smith realized that the concept of "cultural voluntarism" put very little pressure upon lawmakers to enact slave-liberating legislation. Underlying all the bickering between anti-slavery factions, a Constitutional amendment was what both Smith and Garrison wanted. Even John Brown, who never fully understood Smith's lofty ideals, would eventually write his own Provisional Constitution to hurry the abolition of slavery by force of arms.

At first, Smith personified Brown as a missionary for his experimental community of blacks in Essex County, and Brown intended for Smith to think of him in that way. But in Massachusetts he walked the streets of Springfield, mingled with black families, and talked of violence. His law was a Higher Law. Other people just got in the way and complicated everything with compromise. He had no money, but Gerrit Smith did. Some day Mr. Smith would understand the remarkable influence of violence, sniff the danger and excitement, and open his purse.

After his visit to Peterboro John Brown could no longer focus his energies on the affairs of Perkins & Brown. He felt drawn to the rocky slopes of North Elba, and in the fall of 1848 he packed his bags, transferred temporary control of the business to John Jr., and headed for Essex County. He followed the Ausable River into Keene, New York, and then plunged westward through a valley leading to Lake Placid. All about him were the peaks of the Adirondacks, the genesis of the great Appalachian range which swept southward, and would serve as a refuge for his army of liberators. The expansive wilderness country stirred his senses. Never before had he felt so "keenly alive" but at the same time so aware of the insignificance of his existence.[15]

As he descended a hill, he saw a small colony of ten black families, each with forty acres of partially cleared land still littered with rocks too large to move. In the center of the colony fluttered a ragged red flag with the inscription "Timbucto." The few white settlers with small farms on the surrounding hillsides avoided the settlement, but Brown went from cabin to cabin. He passed through little shanties "built of logs with flat roofs out of which little stove pipes protruded," and assured each family that he would live among them and bring them help.[16] He walked their fields and gave them advice. John Brown could see that Smith's ragged settlers had much to learn about living in the hostile climate of Essex County. To his father he wrote: "I can think of no place where I think I would sooner go, all things considered than to live with those poor despised Africans to try, & encourage them; & show them a little so far as I am capable how to manage."[17]

Brown returned to Springfield refreshed and excited, only to be confronted by more bad news. Perkins & Brown would lose $8,000.00 in 1848. During the year 130,000 pounds of wool had been sorted, graded, bundled, and stacked in the warehouse. With the price of wool averaging less than 39 cents a pound, sales receipts totaled $50,000.00. Huge piles of fleece still lay unsold, and he fumed silently at the buyers for not paying his price. If necessary, he would ship it to England and obtain fair value. But for the moment, he could only think of his desire to be among the blacks of Essex County, to settle his family on his own land, and to work out the final threads of his destiny.[18]

John Jr., who tried with patience and diligence to keep accounts straight, objected when his father dipped into the partnership's borrowed cash and sent five barrels of pork and five barrels of flour to the black farmers of "Timbucto." The supplies were forwarded to Willis A. Hodges, who was active in settling blacks on Smith's forty acre plots. Brown wrote: "Say to my colored friends with you that they will be no losers by keeping their patience...They can busy themselves in cutting plenty of hard wood and in getting any kind of work they can find until spring...Do not let anyone forget the vast importance of sustaining the very best character for honesty, truth, industry and faithfulness...." But for black colonists in Essex County, there was no work. And back in Akron, Ohio, Simon Perkins fretted over a pile of burgeoning debts and began to wonder about the "honesty, truth, industry and faithfulness" of his junior partner.[19]

In the winter of 1849 buyers showed a sudden interest in the partnership's wool. Brown imagined that the mills had finally exhausted their resistance to his "fair" pricing policies. To encourage sales, he even discounted his fine fleece, but the mills were only stalling for time. They had sent agents into the countryside to buy directly from the growers, including Brown's own clients, at prices below the Springfield stock. Eventually, Brown discovered the plot and lowered the price on his poorer grades, but the buyers were not interested. Pressured by his partner, scoffed by his clients, and boycotted by his customers, Brown admitted that the business was failing. He considered packing up his fleece and shipping it to London.[20]

But Brown had other problems and the trip to Europe would have to wait. Ellen, born May 20, 1848, had fallen ill and died in April. Mary and the children were sick. One of his best clerks quit to become a train conductor. The junior partner could not find time to respond to the daily flood of angry letters from growers, attorneys, and Simon Perkins. His head reeled with indecision. If he went to Europe, he was unsure he could count on his son to make the same business decisions he would make. Then, too, there was the promised land in Essex County. If Perkins closed the warehouse, Brown knew that his family's existence depended upon having that land. Would Gerrit Smith still honor the options if he failed to keep his promise to look after the black families in Essex County?

Shaken by recurring attacks of malaria, and faced with another business catastrophe, the despairing wool merchant urged farmers to send their fleece to him and he would sell it at a fair price in Europe. He doubted his own convictions but could think of no other alternative. Going to London would buy time, and maybe something would turn up to his advantage. But Thomas Musgrave, a friendly Englishman employed by a New England knitting mill, warned Brown that British manufacturers held irreversible prejudices against Yankee fleece, and considered it coarse and dirty. Musgrave offered 60 cents a pound for Perkins & Brown's own Saxony clip, a veritable windfall for the troubled wool merchant. But Brown was convinced that he could get a better price in England and sent Musgrave away. Later, as Brown was packing his wool for shipment to England, Aaron Erickson, a wool dealer from western New York, stopped by the warehouse and exhorted Brown to not ship his fleece to England. He explained that fine wool, despite the tariff, was currently being exported from England at lower prices than American wool. But Brown did not listen. He had already informed Perkins and his growers otherwise.[21]

When Brown recovered from malaria, his shoulders were stooped and his usual bright but solemn expression had changed to dour resignation. Perkins had curtailed wool shipments to the warehouse. With the partnership approaching dissolution, Brown could see no financial basis for keeping his family in Springfield. When a smallpox epidemic spread through the town in May, he loaded his wife, two small daughters, Anne, five, and Sarah, two, and all his personal belongings into a large two-wheeled wagon drawn by a single ox. He walked beside the wagon and guided the animal with Ruth, age twenty, on one side, and Oliver, age ten, on the other.

Nearly two weeks passed before they reached a small rented home situated on the road from Keene to Lake Placid. The owner, Mr. Flanders, had grown tired of the hostile climate and moved back to Pennsylvania. When the family pulled up the lane to the tiny bungalow, three of the boys were there to greet them. Owen, twenty-four, Watson, thirteen, and Salmon, twelve, had driven to Essex County a small herd of Devon cattle purchased by their father in Connecticut. John Jr., now twenty-eight, remained in Springfield to run the warehouse. Jason, twenty-six, and Frederick, eighteen, were in Akron caring for the sheep of Perkins & Brown on Mutton Hill. Ruth Brown, who left an account of the family's journey to North Elba, wrote that the house "had one good-sized room below, which answered pretty well for the kitchen, dining-room, and parlor; also a pantry and two bedrooms; and the chamber furnished space for four beds," but when a little colored boy stopped at the gate looking for work, "father hired him to help carry on the farm, so there were ten of us in the little house."[22]

Brown felt pressed to return to Springfield, but first he felt obligated to circulate among Gerrit Smith's black landowners. He discovered many of them had been cheated by a land-surveyor who took advantage of their ignorance and forced them to settle on poor land that did not correspond with Smith's deeds. Brown got out his surveying instruments and started to replot boundaries. When some of the families learned that they had been cheated, they packed their scant belongings and trudged back to the cities. Word spread through the colony, and as new settlers wandered into Essex County to build their shanties and clear their land, they stopped by the Flander's farm to ask for Brown. For two months surveyor Brown was so busy that he barely found time to settle his family and stake-out the 244 acres Smith had sold him for $1 an acre.[23]

In late July, John Brown kissed his wife good-bye and reluctantly returned to the Springfield warehouse. John Jr. had dutifully packed 200,000 pounds of wool into 690 bales and shipped them to London. On August 15, Brown boarded the steamer *Cambria*. As he left Boston, the *Dry Goods Reporter*, a trade paper published in New York, wrote that Brown's wool in London had been sold to American mills at ruinous prices for the partnership's growers. The report, although false, came close to hitting the mark a few weeks later. No sooner had Brown departed for London than the domestic price of fine fleece jumped to over sixty cents a pound. John Jr. nearly emptied the warehouse. He attempted to recall his father but could not reach him. Had Brown been given a moment to reflect, he would have attributed his poor timing to predestination—not bad luck or faulty management.[24]

When Brown arrived in London, he learned that the local wool auction would not be held until mid-September. With time on his hands, he crossed to the mainland, visited Paris, Hamburg, and Brussels, and with the eye of a trained surveyor, he spent a few days studying the battlefield of Waterloo. He returned to England in time to watch 150 bales of his lower grade fleece sell between 26 and 29 cents a pound, compared with 35 cents in Springfield. He withdrew the remaining lots and hoped his fine fleece would do better, but the highest grades sold for 30 to 46 cents a pound, less than half what British mills were paying for their locally grown fleece. Disgusted and humiliated, he withdrew all of the remaining bales from the auction and shipped them back to Springfield. Brown came home with his fleece, convinced that English wool buyers were a pack of ruthless swindlers.[25]

John Jr. tallied up his father's London receipts and reported that the partnership lost a staggering $40,000.00. For John Brown, it was time to face reality. A second round of bankruptcy proceedings loomed in the future, but this time he had a wealthy partner who could cover the losses.

When he met with Simon Perkins in the spring of 1850 to discuss methods for liquidating the business, the senior partner gladly agreed, but he made the mistake of leaving all the details to Brown. Despite the disaster, he still wanted Brown to continue raising his sheep in Akron. Perkins decided to recover his losses by indenturing Brown and his boys to servitude on Mutton Hill. Out of deference to Perkins, Brown agreed. If he was to save the farm in North Elba, and the few possessions he had accumulated in Springfield, he had to avoid bankruptcy. At the age of fifty, nothing scared him more.[26]

For nearly four years, Brown circulated back and forth between Springfield, North Elba and Akron, trying to keep his family together while settling accounts, defending lawsuits and pressing counter-suits. He had no peace, and no contact with Gerrit Smith in Peterboro, New York. But in 1850, events having nothing to do with Brown's financial imbroglio began bringing the wool merchant and the philanthropist together again.

The passage of the Compromise of 1850 and the Fugitive Slave Act incensed Gerrit Smith and reawakened latent militant thoughts in the mind of John Brown. In January, 1850, Senator James M. Mason of Virginia had introduced a bill to provide for "the more faithful execution of the clause in the Constitution requiring the return of fugitive slaves." About the same time, 72-year old Kentucky Senator Henry Clay placed before Congress several provisions intended to placate sectional differences. With help from Senator Stephen A. Douglas, a politically brilliant compromise was shepherded through the legislative process. The basic components of the package provided for the admission of California as a free state, the organization of the territories of Utah and New Mexico without reference to slavery, the prohibition of the slave trade in the District of Columbia, the payment of Texas public debt and settlement of Texas boundaries, and the passage of the new Fugitive Slave Act. After months of fierce debate, Congress, believing it had solved the nation's problems, passed both bills in September. Smith, who had previously rejected many opportunities to seek political office, suddenly agreed to run for Congress as an antislavery independent. By a thin plurality, indignant New York voters sent Smith to Congress.[27]

The new Fugitive Slave Act created an angry reaction in the North. In 1793 Congress had passed the first fugitive slave law as a means to protect Southern "property" rights in chattel slavery. Eventually, Northern states began to abolish slavery and passed personal liberty laws to safeguard free blacks. Over time, this legislation rendered the old law useless. Under the new law, Northern officials were compelled to return a slave to his owner. Any person found guilty of assisting a fugitive was subject to six months imprisonment, a $1,000.00 fine, and reimbursement to the owner the market value of the slave. The law denied fugitives a jury trial and protection under a writ of habeas corpus. Many Northerners regarded the law as a flagrant violation of fundamental American rights and wanted new personal liberty laws enacted to weaken the 1850 Act. Congressmen who believed the new fugitive slave law would relieve sectional tensions discovered that they had accomplished the opposite. Antislavery organizations attracted thousands of new members, and men like Gerrit Smith and John Brown deliberately violated the legislation.

Brown, who believed nothing could be settled by compromise, agonized over the act and set time aside time to fight it in his own way. With visions of slavecatchers, reinforced by constables and federal marshals invading Springfield and North Elba in search of his black friends, Brown wrote his wife, "It now seems that the Fugitive Slave Law was to be the means of making more Abolitionists than all the lectures we have had for years. It really looks as if God had his hand on this wickedness....I of course keep encouraging my colored friends to trust in God, and keep their powder dry. I did so today, at Thanksgiving meeting, publicly..."[28]

Smith's convictions received a test several weeks before he was officially seated in the House. A close friend, William L. Chaplin, general agent of the New York Anti-Slavery Society, editor of the Albany *Patriot*, and a man of remarkable intelligence, ignored Smith's warning, traveled to Washington, and participated in the heist of two slaves belonging to Congressmen Robert Toombs and Alexander H. Stephens. Captured and thrown into prison, Chaplin and two co-conspirators were released five months later on $25,000.00 bail. Smith helped put up the bail, but with mixed-feelings he agreed with the other bondsmen that since conviction was certain, the bail should be forfeited. He paid his share, but not without grumbling, "I am robbed of these twelve thousand dollars; I have been robbed of a great deal from time to time, in the sums which I have felt myself morally compelled to pay in the purchase of the liberty of slaves. I greatly needed all this money to expend in other directions."[29]

Anxious to expiate the guilt of his great wealth, Smith put more than money into his fight against slavery. During a convention of the Liberty Party in Syracuse, October 1, 1851, the alarm bell tolled, alerting the town's Vigilance Committee that a black man had been seized under the Fugitive Slave Act. Smith interrupted the convention, organized a group of followers, and descended upon the city jail where Jerry McHenry, who had been pinioned to the floor of a wagon by two policemen, was being dragged into a cell. A crowd stood outside the jail and threatened to break down the doors. The trembling fugitive, hearing the uproar, expected imminent death—not deliverance. But Smith came on the field with a battering ram and led a band of refined but earnest preachers, free blacks, antislavery workers and farmers against the flimsy door of the jail. They broke it down, captured the police, smashed open the cell, led Jerry to a light carriage drawn by a span of fleet horses, thrust money into his hand, and sent him streaking through the night to Canada.[30]

For most of his career, Daniel Webster had fought slavery, but in 1850 he compromised to preserve the Union by supporting the Fugitive Slave Act. He turned up at the Syracuse convention, stood before the hostile group, and in his great commanding voice defended the law. "Depend upon it," he declared, "the law will be executed in its spirit and to its letter. It will be executed in all the great cities— here in Syracuse—in the midst of the next Anti-Slavery Convention, if the occasion shall arise. Then we shall see what becomes of their lives and their sacred honor."[31]

After the Jerry McHenry rescue, Gerrit Smith spoke to the convention and delivered his answer to Daniel Webster, referring to him as "that base and infamous enemy of the human race." After a one-sided demeaning assault on Webster's character, Smith introduced a series of resolutions defying "the satanic prediction of the satanic Daniel Webster" and obliterating "the influence of the devil-prompted speeches of politicians and devil-prompted sermons of priests." During the presentation, Smith demonstrated emotion bordering on fanaticism, for under that veneer of wealth and substance was a man who could be driven to break laws and instigate precipitous action. That day in Syracuse, he rocked the convention with his words. For some years thereafter, the people of the city invited him to preside at an annual dinner to celebrate the anniversary of Jerry McHenry's deliverance.[32]

In Springfield, Brown had not been idle. With part of his family in North Elba and the rest in Akron, he had spent his evenings organizing the black community to resist the fugitive slave law. After spending much of his life trying to unscramble the mysteries of the Old Testament, his mind had become fixed on the Book of Judges, and how Gideon, with a small force backed by the Lord's blessing, rescued Israel from a host of Midianites in the battle of Mount Gilead. The more he deliberated on "The sword of the Lord, and of Gideon," the more convinced he became that God's special message to him lay in those few passages of scripture. With inescapable business problems demanding his time, he could not travel south and slice out the heart of slavery. But he could organize the black community in Springfield to defend themselves against slavecatchers and prevent the return of fugitives to the South.[33]

When a runaway was captured in New York and returned to his master, blacks became terrified, especially after they learned that free blacks were also being snatched from the streets and transported south. In Springfield, blacks could not sleep, certain that slavecatchers lurked in the shadows and would come in the night to capture husbands, wives and children, and drag them away in chains. Brown encouraged them to resist and to defend their homes and families. He was fighting mad and his anger drew them together. In January he composed a remarkable document and gathered his black friends for a reading of "Words of Advice." He followed the reading by rallying his listeners together and establishing on the 15th the first branch of the United States League of Gileadites. "Union is Strength" became Brown's theme, as he encouraged his black neighbors to arm themselves and use their weapons if threatened by slavecatchers.[34]

Brown, posing as a negro author, had published an earlier tract titled *Sambo's Mistakes*, in which he alluded to the perceived deficiencies in the black culture—besides a chronic good nature. Sambo had been taught to read but wasted his time on silly novels and other useless trash. Drinking, smoking and chewing tobacco had taken his money, which could have been better spent on buying a farm, starting a library, or helping others of his race. Sambo had succumbed to self-indulgence, and had become so impressed by his sprouting talents that he failed to work with fellow abolitionists whenever a crisis threatened his freedom. Sambo erred by believing that the favor of whites could be cultivated by "tamely submitting to every species of indignity instead of nobly resisting their brutal aggressions...."[35]

Accordingly, Brown opened his "Words of Advice" with the statement, "Nothing so charms the American people as personal bravery. The trial for life of one bold and to some extent successful man, for defending his rights in good earnest, would arouse more sympathy throughout the nation than the accumulated wrongs and sufferings of more than three millions of our submissive colored population." He told them to not be submissive, to arm and defend themselves. He urged them to not "do your work by halves, but make clean work with your enemies," and above all, "Stand by one another and by your friends, while a drop of blood remains; and be hanged, if you must, but tell no tales out of school. Make no confession."[36]

Forty-four black men and women joined Brown's first and only League of the Gileadites. His hope of expanding the League through the abolition states of America never materialized, but the exercise strengthened his personal resolve to wage war against the fugitive slave law and destroy, if possible, the "peculiar institution" itself.

For three more years, he struggled to salvage his home and his reputation. He had little time and no money to invest in the cause of freedom. After moving his family back to Ohio where he could care for them, he finally placated Simon Perkins. In a gesture of either generosity or good riddance, Perkins gave Brown a small settlement in cash in December, 1854.

The ex-wool merchant's older boys decided to go to Kansas. They begged him to go with them, but John Brown was fifty-four years old, tired, discouraged, and still indebted to Gerrit Smith. Henry Thompson, daughter Ruth's husband, had built a snug home for the Brown family in North Elba. The old man remembered how he once wanted to "rest his bones" among "God's omnipotence," and with his family now transplanted back in Essex County, New York, he decided to go there and live out his life among the needy blacks.[37]

While Brown struggled to overcome his misfortunes, Gerrit Smith spent an inconspicuous term in Congress. He made speeches that nobody listened to and preached against the use of intoxicating drinks in the nation's capital—where wine and whiskey flowed as freely as gossip. In Washington, he entertained often with lavish dinners, but served only tea, coffee, or lemonade. He spoke earnestly against slavery, and shared his opinions on war, finance, temperance and government. His peers considered his ideas visionary, peculiar, harmless and impractical. The Chicago *Tribune* called him "a wrong headed fanatic, wilful and intractable, conceited and wayward, whose intellect ran to paradox, whose wisdom was akin to folly, and who injured his side more than the opposition."[38] At the end of one session, Smith resigned and returned to Peterboro. He had better things to do.

In Congress, Smith never changed, remaining an affable country gentleman with money but no aptitude for peddling political influence. Those who knew him well recognized this. His many associates considered him to be, among other things, eccentric, emotional, unpredictable, ambivalent and generous. John Brown, who entered the wealthy abolitionist's Peterboro mansion in 1848, was only one of the many people who would learn how to manipulate the magnanimous Mr. Smith. [39]

3

Kansas Crusaders

When Gerrit Smith took his seat in Congress on December 12, 1853, Southern legislators were beginning to debate territorial issues unresolved by the Compromise of 1850. By precedent, the new law provided inhabitants of the Great Plains territorial discretion over slavery without repealing the Missouri Compromise of 1820, which had designated land below latitude 36 degrees 30' (and would have excluded Kansas) as open to slavery. The law was intended to allow an equal balance of power between slave and free states. Settlers were moving to the Plains, however, and the South feared that by allowing Northern proponents to establish two new territories, Kansas and Nebraska, above the arbitrary line created by the Missouri Compromise, slave interests would lose their political equilibrium. They also worried that if Kansas abolished slavery, Missouri, a slave-state, would be geographically surrounded on all sides by free states. Southern legislators, aware of the hopelessness of mandating Kansas a slave state, demanded that the 36 degree 30' boundary be removed, thereby enabling the inhabitants of Missouri, who had much at stake, to coerce Kansas settlers and bring the new territory into the Union as slave.

Senator Stephen A. Douglas of Illinois, who had given strong support to the Compromise of 1850, introduced the Kansas-Nebraska Bill. This nullified the old boundary and allowed the people of the two new territories to decide the slave issue by popular sovereignty. Douglas had more interest in railroads than slavery. He saw an opportunity for Chicago to become the hub for a trans-continental railroad. He also had presidential aspirations and wished to ingratiate himself with Southern voters. Douglas believed the plains presented a natural barrier to the expansion of slavery, but he underestimated the volatile impact of the Kansas-Nebraska Act upon Northern free-soilers.

Many Southerners doubted if Kansas would become a slave state, but they wanted legislative barriers removed which implied slavery was an undesirable institution. They looked beyond Kansas and Nebraska and wanted unrestricted access to future territorial acquisitions, such as Cuba and Mexico. President Franklin Pierce encouraged his fellow Democrats to vote for the bill, but before it passed, abolitionists had their say. On April 6, 1854, Gerrit Smith spoke to Congress, demanding, "No slavery in Nebraska; no slavery in the nation...." Like all of Smith's speeches, it did no good.[1]

Pierce's election in the fall of 1852 had demolished the Whig Party, and the Democrats controlled the government. When the Kansas-Nebraska Act passed on May 30, 1854, after five months of bitter debate, some Southerners believed they had won an unwritten understanding that Kansas would enter the Union as a slave state and Nebraska as a free state, thereby maintaining the cherished political balance. But neither Douglas nor his Southern supporters anticipated the events which followed the passage of the bill. Free-soil advocates suddenly multiplied in number, leading to political chaos in the North. Former Whigs and Democrats joined the rapidly growing Republican Party as their only political alternative. Republican leadership was not anti-slavery, but they opposed the further expansion of slavery as immoral and an infringement on opportunities for free-white labor. At the same time, wealthy Northern abolitionists financed families willing to settle in Kansas and vote for free-state status. The struggle for control of Kansas erupted into a tragic intercine conflict known thereafter as "Bleeding Kansas." In different ways, John Brown and Gerrit Smith became participants in the conflict.[2]

In 1854, Brown's two oldest boys, John Jr., age thirty-three, and Jason, age thirty-one, owned farms in Ohio. Three younger boys, Owen, twenty-nine, Frederick, twenty-three, and Salmon, seventeen, worked Perkins & Brown's sheep farm and helped their older brothers plant and harvest. But there would be no harvest in 1854. A hot summer drought scorched the land; leaves dropped from the trees, unripened fruit shriveled to mush, corn wilted in the fields, and farmers barely made an early crop of hay. By mid-summer, northern Ohio became a desert without water. The lure of cheap land in Kansas became compelling, especially to John Brown, Jr., who wrote "most of the Northern newspapers were not only full of glowing accounts of the extraordinary fertility, healthfulness, and beauty of the Territory of Kansas...newly opened for settlement, but of urgent appeals to all lovers of freedom who desired homes in a new region to go there as settlers, and by their votes save Kansas from the curse of slavery."[3]

The Brown boys manifested some of their father's gravitation to riches and liberty, and Ohio's drought had left them with unpaid debts and not much hope. Sam and Florilla Adair, John Brown's half sister, had already migrated to Kansas, built a cabin outside Osawatomie, and encouraged the boys to come west. John Jr., although he had a mind of his own, wanted his father to come with him, settle in Kansas, fight for the free-state cause, and move the family to a gentler climate.[4]

But Brown Sr. was not ready for a move. He had become a prisoner of his own indecision and captive to his own economic plight. He wrote to Smith for advice, a rare request from a man who kept his own counsel. The Peterboro landowner expressed a wish that the weary shepherd return to North Elba to look after his flock of black settlers. Brown had reached a crossroad somewhere between old age and youthful aspiration, and he did not know what to do. He no longer held half interest in the Perkins & Brown flock; all title and remaining debts had reverted to the senior partner. The two Ohio farms he had leased and planted in the summer of 1854 were wiped out by the same drought that destroyed the crops of his sons. The only property he now owned lay on the stark, untilled hillsides of North Elba. For a while, he remained in Ohio, too poor to move his family home. If Brown considered going to Kansas in the spring of 1855, he had no money to do so—at least, not yet.[5] In June, he sold his small herd of cattle, packed the family belongings into carts, and returned to the Adirondacks. They moved into a crude, unplastered four room home built by son-in-law Henry Thompson.[6]

Brown had barely settled in North Elba when letters of distress started to arrive from Kansas. John Jr., Jason, and their families had been harassed by pro-slavery ruffians during their trip across Missouri, Jason's son Austin had died of cholera, and the boys were nearly out of money. When they reached their tracts on North Middle Creek and started to cut hay and plant corn, malarial fevers invaded the camp-site and laid everyone low. Hay rotted in the fields, and with no time to build fences, cattle strayed away. They pitched tents and lived in the open, too sick to build cabins.[7]

During the spring elections in Kansas, thousands of Missourians crossed the border and cast votes for pro-slavery candidates. A small number of elected free-soilers were bullied and ousted from the first legislative meetings. Angry Kansas settlers met in a separate convention, repudiated the fraudulently chosen legislature, and refused to obey its enactments. Armed Missourians crossed the border to enforce the laws of the bogus legislature and drive off the rebellious free-state farmers. Eight well-armed riders, led by Reverend Martin White, trotted into Brown's Station during dinner and demanded to know the family's stand on slavery. "We are Free State," they answered, "and more than that we are abolitionists." White's irregulars responded with threats and rode off. John Jr. surmised that Brown's Station, along with the lives of those upon it, were marked for destruction. Smarting from the potential injustice of being driven off his land, and fearing for his life, John, Jr. sent his father a lengthy letter asking for revolvers and rifles. "The Antislavery portion of the inhabitants should immediately...arm and organize themselves in military companies," John Jr. wrote. "Now we want you to get for us these arms. We need them more than we do bread. Would not Gerrit Smith...furnish the money and loan it to us...until we can raise enough to refund it from the Free soil of Kansas?" The elder Brown no doubt recognized some of the same language he had used in organizing the Gileadites by exhorting his black friends to kill anybody who tried to enforce the fugitive slave law.[8]

Brown pictured a massive army of pro-slavery border ruffians raiding Kansas farmlands, burning out settlers, pillaging homes and carrying off stock. The image stirred memories of slavecatchers roaming the streets of Springfield searching for runaways and terrifying his black friends. Although he had told his son earlier that he felt committed to operate against Satan and his legions "in another part of the field," he felt suddenly drawn to Kansas. A letter from Salmon offered great incentive: "Kansas is the greatest country to make money in, that I ever saw," and he encouraged the entire family to come to the territory.[9]

Brown was not the sort of person to ignore prospects for money, but the letter from John Jr. meant much more to him than Salmon's enthusiastic invitation. Gerrit Smith was at a convention of Radical Political Abolitionists in Syracuse with Frederick

Douglass, Samuel J. May, Lewis Tappan and other activists who called for the Federal government to suppress slavery and prevent the return of runaway slaves. They had just pledged more than $4600.00 to finance their crusade when on June 28, 1855, Brown sauntered into convention hall with John Jr.'s appeal for arms. He argued that free-soil settlers in Kansas needed money to buy guns to defend themselves against the armies of evil massed along the Missouri border. Would the convention contribute money for weapons so he could go to Kansas and help his sons fight for freedom? Most of the delegates wanted to defeat slavery through the political process and were not anxious to support bloodshed in faraway Kansas, but Smith and Douglass took the podium and spoke in Brown's behalf. Smith read John Jr.'s letters "with such effect as to draw tears from the numerous eyes in the great collection of people present." Smith passed the hat, and when it came back he counted out a trifling forty dollars. Somewhat apologetically, he pressed another $20 into Brown's hand. But the slim, gaunt farmer from North Elba was pleased. On his way west he would stop in Akron and other towns where he was known and raise more money, money with no strings attached. And Gerrit Smith, who shed a few tears himself, had opened his purse once and would do it again.[10]

John Brown traveled to Kansas with son-in-law Henry Thompson in a one-horse wagon loaded with rifles, revolvers and two-edged broadswords. Meanwhile, Gerrit Smith put the self-styled Gideon out of his mind and returned to the task of achieving emancipation by political means. He wrote to arch-abolitionist Wendell Phillips and complained that anti-slavery organizations were not unified. He added that they bickered too much among themselves, and had accomplished little aside from winning the contempt of all slaveholders. In August, 1857, he spoke at the National Compensation Convention in Cleveland and supported the proposal that "the North ought to share with the South in the temporary losses that will result from the abolition of slavery." However, even Gerrit Smith could not make up his mind on the ultimate solution to end slavery, and he attached himself to any new proposal short of outright violence.[11]

In November, 1855, Eli Thayer began an intensive campaign to raise fresh funds so the New England Emigrant Aid Company could underwrite the cost of sending more free-soil settlers to Kansas. The Emigrant Aid Company, formed in April 1854, one month prior to the passage of the Kansas-Nebraska Act, had been salting the territory with free-soil voters for over a year. Pro-slavery interests were now no longer content to fight back by stuffing ballot boxes. Armed disruptions spread through the plains. Reports drifted east of the "Wakarusa war," a brush between free-state advocates and three thousand armed Missourians who wanted to burn Lawrence, Kansas, the principal center of free-soil resistance. At the time, neither Thayer nor Smith knew that John Brown was there with the boys and the family's wagon-load of rifles, revolvers and broadswords.[12]

Nothing stirred Northern hostility more than Missourians mixing into Kansas affairs. Moderate-minded citizens, including Gerrit Smith, dipped into their pockets and contributed thousands of dollars to the Emigrant Aid Society. Fund-raisers traveled through New York, stopping in Peterboro and Syracuse. Smith, who had spoken consistently against violence, contributed one hundred dollars. By early 1856, and now aware of the likelihood of bloodshed since murders had already been committed, Smith sent $250.00 to Amos Lawrence, treasurer of the Emigrant Aid Society. Lawrence, respecting Smith's professed convictions, wrote, "I have thought that the money spent in rifles has done the most good thus far, and may appropriate yours in that way, unless you object." Smith authorized Lawrence to use the money as he saw fit, adding: "Much as I abhor war, I nevertheless believe, that there are instances in which the shedding of blood is unavoidable." Lawrence responded, assuring Smith that the guns would not be used against the Federal government.[13] Just six months earlier, Smith had refused to buy guns, writing to a boy's military company in Washington, "I am so afraid of war and patriotism, that I dare not buy one musket..."[14]

Smith's small contribution to Lawrence's weapons fund was only the beginning of his commitment to violence. Free-soil advocates in Albany organized a Kansas Aid Committee and invited Smith to deliver one of five keynote addresses at their March 13 convention. When Eli Thayer heard of the meeting, he agreed to be present, and tactfully hoped to secure a few dollars for his own organization. Smith wrote a flurry of letters to influential associates encouraging them to come to Albany. Most of them attended and heard the man from Peterboro condemn the repeal of the Missouri Compromise as "perfidious and very wicked," and then lash out at "the unmitigated and desperate scoundrels in Missouri" who were out to make Kansas a slave state. He expressed his worries that innocent settlers were being coerced to submit to "this ruffian government." With unusual vehemence he declared: "But in no event must they submit to it. They must resist it, even if doing so they have to resist both Congress and the President. And we must stand by them in their resistance."[15]

Moderate Mr. Smith had now gone almost full circle, stopping just short of disunion, treason and civil war. At the close of the convention, the treasurer announced that cash and subscriptions totaled $4,940.00. Gerrit Smith, who hesitatingly gave John Brown $20.00 nine months earlier, subscribed and paid $3,000.00. He returned to Peterboro and assumed the leadership for raising pledges in Madison and Jefferson counties. He contributed liberally to people who promised to go to Kansas and take up permanent residency. By the middle of April, 1856, he wrote to a friend: "I haven't a spare dollar. I am using all the money I can lay hold of to send good families to Kansas, and help secure that Territory to Freedom." John Brown, whose timing concerning money matters was always notoriously poor, had left for Kansas too soon.[16]

Gerrit Smith may have temporarily drained his cash resources but not his commitment. Free-soil advocate Andrew H. Reeder, the deposed territorial governor of Kansas, came east and proposed that funds be raised to place five thousand armed settlers in Kansas. He suggested the formation of the National Kansas Committee, with headquarters in Chicago, and urged that two million dollars be raised to support the effort. On July 9, 1856, fifty-six delegates met at Buffalo. The militant majority, men like Gerrit Smith, Eli Thayer, Dr. Samuel Gridley Howe, William Barnes and Thaddeus Hyatt, gave less militant members like Abraham Lincoln little time to express their views. Smith presented four resolutions, two shocking enough to provoke a heated discussion. The first asked that "armed men...be sent to Kansas to conquer the armed men who came against her...." The second demanded that any attempt to impose slavery upon Kansas be defeated by force "at whatever cost...whether the Administration shall, or shall not, continue to favor the nefarious attempt."[17]

Not all delegates agreed with Smith's bloodthirsty proposals. A committee of seven, including both Smith and Thayer, toned down the resolutions, created the National Kansas Committee, and appointed Eli Thayer as General Agent "to perfect the organization of the various States." When the call came for contributions, Smith dug deeply into the bottoms of his silver-lined pockets and pledged $1,500.00 a month for the duration of the "present contest."[18]

With Kansas already "bleeding" on a small scale, and with Smith's belligerent resolutions circulating and finding acceptance in the North, conscientious Americans might have shuddered at the prospect of "what next?" Smith, not clearly realizing that his radical militant actions could lead to disunion, placed the blame upon the slaveholder. In a letter to Ohio Congressman Joshua Giddings, Smith wrote that "there is reason to fear that our Government is rapidly drawing to its close. The encroachments and outrages of the slave-power on the one hand, and the base submission to them on the other have apparently brought us to a period of the breaking up of the nation."[19]

Gerrit Smith, who lived comfortably in his Peterboro mansion, could speak of "Bleeding Kansas," pass resolutions, contribute money, write letters, foment disunion, and agitate the South from the security of his well-appointed parlor. If return on money invested in the territory could be measured in blood, Smith made a very good investment. So did several others who dribbled coins into a passing hat that warm day in June when Brown stopped in Syracuse on his way to Kansas. Smith could also be certain that the somber patriarch at Brown's Station had followed with interest the organization of the National Kansas Committee and had not underestimated or overlooked the generosity of his friend in Peterboro. One day soon, Brown would want his reward.

Unlike the sons who had preceded him to Kansas, when Brown left Chicago with Henry Thompson and his one horse wagon, he carried no farming implements or young fruit trees to start an orchard. Aside from a few supplies, only rifles, revolvers, broadswords, and surveying instruments rattled in the heavy crates that bumped along the dusty roads leading west. "Give us arms, and we are ready for the contest," John Jr. had said. There was not room or money for the pork, meal and beans Salmon had requested. But Brown had his own reasons for going to Kansas. He still wanted to be in charge, and even at the age of fifty-five he had his eyes open and wanted "to see if something would not turn up to his advantage."[20]

When he reached Brown's Station in October, 1855, he found everyone sick, no winter shelters built, crops unpicked, cattle unattended, and his sons in despair. "We had, between us all," Brown claimed, "sixty cents in cash." For two months he nursed the family back to health, built cabins, gathered provisions, and with help from Sam and Florilla Adair, prepared for winter.

In the evenings the old man and the boys huddled around campfires and talked politics. By December, John Brown knew a little about his neighbors, his free-state friends and his pro-slavery enemies. The slavery issue had little to do with slaves in Kansas; there were few in the Territory. Many free-soil and pro-slavery settlers had moved to Kansas for the same reason. They had no use for the blacks, free or slave, and did not want them as neighbors. The first emigrants allied themselves with Southern interests simply because they believed the pro-slavery party stood for law and order and their farms and possessions would be protected.[21]

Until 1855, militia and armed intrusions from Missouri had kept the peace by intimidating free-soil farmers and stuffing ballot boxes. When the New England Emigrant Aid Society started to send settlers to Kansas, the balance of political power began to shift away from Missouri's control of the elections. Southerners worried that if they lost control, Kansas would apply to Congress for admission as a free state. Following the example of the emigrant aid companies of the North, the South began to raise money and on a much smaller scale financed the relocation of families from Alabama and Georgia to Kansas. But farmers who once brought only axes, plows, livestock and an old fowling piece, now brought rifles, revolvers and Bowie knives. For a person who came to Kansas to see if something might turn up to his advantage, John Brown had come at the right time. Politics, not slaves, turned the Territory into a setting for civil war. In the first election held on November 24, 1854, Missourians crossed into Kansas, cast 1,729 pro-slavery votes, and successfully seated their hand-picked delegates to Congress. In March, 1855, when Territorial Governor Andrew H. Reeder called for a general election to select the first legislature, Missourians crowded into wagons, rode by Reeder's home flourishing whiskey bottles, and cast their votes. That evening, having done their patriotic duty, they rumbled back home. Of 6,307 votes cast, nearly five-sixths were those of the invaders. Reeder unseated seven pro-slavery men for "technical flaws," but on the first pass, representatives of the South won thirty-eight of thirty-nine seats. In a later election, the seven empty seats were filled by free-soil men, but they were physically ejected by the pro-slavery majority at the first meeting of the legislature.[22]

Terrorization of free-soil settlers followed on the heels of the elections. Emigrants passing through Missouri on their way to Kansas were threatened, robbed, beaten, and in some cases, thrown off river boats carrying them up the Missouri River to Kansas. People like John Jr. who came to Kansas to settle wrote angry letters home asking for guns. In Kansas, Dr. Charles Robinson became the unofficial free-state spokesman. Fiery James H. Lane, who had political aspirations of his own, connected himself with the free-state cause and became Robinson's right-hand man. Robinson and Lane set up headquarters in Lawrence, the unofficial free-state capital of Kansas. From there, they conspired against the illegitimately elected pro-slavery legislature which was enacting "bogus" laws at nearby Shawnee Mission, close to the protection of the Missouri border. It was Robinson who wrote to the Emigrant Aid Society requesting rifles, and through his agent, George W. Deitzler, convinced people like Gerrit Smith and Eli Thayer to spend thousands of dollars on arms and ammunition. To disguise shipments, carefully packed crates containing guns flowed westward marked "Beecher's Bibles."[23]

By the time Brown reached Kansas, free-soil settlers were beginning to shoot back at border ruffians, and the conflict manifested signs of ballooning into open warfare. John Jr. had been chosen as a free-state delegate to help write a state constitution and apply for admission to the Union. Pro-slavery settlers living near Brown's Station distrusted the clan, and when Brown, Sr. arrived with a small arsenal, they branded the family as trouble-makers. People like William and "Dutch" Henry Sherman, who owned a large store on the California Road, and Allen Wilkinson, who had been elected to the pro-slavery legislature by 150 illegal votes, did not want the militant Browns disrupting their political supremacy.[24]

The killings started in earnest in October when Samuel Collins, a pro-slavery man, shot Patrick Laughlin for political differences. A month later, Jacob Branson attended a free-state meeting to protest the crime and bring Collins, the alleged murderer, to justice. Samuel J. Jones, a Westport, Missouri, postmaster who had been appointed sheriff of Douglas County, Kansas, crossed the border to arrest Branson for stirring up trouble. Branson was rescued by his friends, and Jones' posse left Lawrence at gunpoint. The Branson rescue gave Jones his long-awaited opportunity to mass a force against Lawrence and destroy the heart of free-state resistance. He asked Governor Wilson Shannon for three thousand troops so he could serve his warrants, and at the end of November hundreds of men crossed from Missouri into Kansas and pitched camp along the Wakarusa River.[25]

John Brown and his boys arrived in Lawrence just after Thomas W. Barber, an unarmed free-soil farmer, had been murdered outside town. They entered the Free-State Hotel and found Robinson and Lane negotiating a peace settlement with Governor Shannon. Brown wanted to fight, but Robinson had matters under control and temporarily prevented further killings. The Missourians returned home vowing to return, and for his willingness to defend Lawrence, Brown became captain of a militia company called the Liberty Guards.

Through the winter and early spring of 1856, news dribbled into Brown's Station of new killings, all free-state men. Brown itched to even the score, and the impetus came by way of a messenger galloping through the countryside shouting that Sheriff Jones' ruffians, backed by Federal forces, had surrounded Lawrence and an attack was imminent. The Liberty Guards formed at Osawatomie and started up the California Road to Lawrence. Half way there, another messenger stopped the company. He warned that the bridge over the Wakarusa was blocked, and Brown was too late to save the town.

John Brown had no report of casualties, but prior to the sacking of Lawrence he had counted six murders of free-state men. Separating from the main body of the Liberty Guards, he formed a small squad of avengers consisting of Owen, Oliver, Salmon, Frederick, Henry Thompson, John Townsley, a local farmer, and Theodore Weiner, a burly Austrian with a small store on Mosquito Creek. Just before midnight on May 25, Brown's men came out of the woods and evened the score. With double-edged broadswords, they sliced to pieces James P. Doyle and two of his boys, William and Drury. They made two more stops, killing Allen Wilkinson and William Sherman, all pro-slavery men who wielded influence among the settlers on Pottawatomie Creek. John Brown fired one symbolic shot, putting a bullet into the head of James Doyle after he died from sword wounds.[26]

By murdering five men, John Brown attempted to demonstrate that free-soil men were willing to fight back, but he and his men were shunned by free-state friends and hunted by enemies. John Jr. and Jason, who had no hand in the murders, were captured by posses, beaten, and dragged to jail in chains, where they narrowly escaped being hanged. They were eventually released, but Brown and his men became hunted renegades, forced to live off the land, heroes to some and villains to others. The man who came to Kansas to see "if something might turn up to his advantage" now had something he wanted—a reputation.

When a company of twenty-five Missourians hunting the Pottawatomie murderers camped at Black Jack Springs, Brown attacked them at sunrise on June 2, and with eight men forced them to surrender. Word of the victory spread through eastern Kansas like wildfire and every renegade in the Territory picked up his rifle and joined "Old Brown's" army. The governor called out federal troops and ordered all unauthorized military groups disbanded. Colonel Edwin V. Sumner's U. S. Dragoons rode into Brown's fort and dispersed about fifty guerrillas. Brown would not fire on the federal government, but a deputy marshal riding with Sumner took one look at the fiery old man, lost his courage, and failed to issue writs for his arrest. Disgusted with the squeamish deputy, Colonel Sumner rode off with his dragoons, leaving Brown at large and still dangerous.[27]

Brown's boys had had enough and wanted to go home. The fifty-six year old patriarch reluctantly agreed, but when they passed through Lawrence, people crowded into the streets to praise the old warrior. The Pottawatomie murders worried him, but now he heard words of vindication. When he reached the Nebraska line, a long line of armed free-state men cheered him as they passed on the road to General Jim Lane's army. John Brown could not go home, not now. But only Frederick stayed with him, and together they marched into Jim Lane's camp.

Lane, whose main interest in life was himself, had lost favor with the National Kansas Committee. About this time Thaddeus Hyatt and Dr. Samuel Gridley Howe, who had raised $110,000.00 in cash and clothing, including $10,000.00 of Gerrit Smith's money, came west to see how the Committee's funds were being spent.[28] Brown trundled into camp about the time Lane was being told by Hyatt and Howe that the Committee did not want civil war in the Territory. They wanted their settlers to cross peacefully into Kansas, establish homes and farms, and vote for freedom in the next election. Brown convinced Hyatt and Howe that his only motive had been to protect the settlers from raiders. A week later he was back in Kansas with a new suit, a fine wagon with a span of four horses, new followers, and some of the Committee's money in his pocket.[29]

In August Brown organized two companies of mounted irregulars. They initiated raids on pro-slavery farmers in Linn County, and drove hundreds of their livestock into the hills north of Osawatomie. Militia General John W. Reid, a Mexican War veteran, started with a force of 250 pro-slavery volunteers to wipe out Osawatomie, John Brown's raiders, and every vestige of free-soil resistance. On the morning of August 30, Reid attacked in force. Brown gathered about twenty-five men and rushed across the river to save the town. After a stiff defense, he gave way to overwhelming odds, and his men fled and disappeared. From a hill overlooking the town, Brown watched Reid's men torch Osawatomie and recapture the rustled cattle. He received a worse shock when he learned that Frederick Brown had been murdered by Reverend White. Once again the grim fighter was reduced to misery and humiliating poverty.[30]

By now, President Pierce had reached the end of his patience with Kansas affairs. For Pierce and the Democrats, the violence in Kansas had become politically costly in the North. He removed Shannon and appointed a new territorial governor, John W. Geary, who vowed to end all guerilla warfare. In his first official proclamation, Geary disbanded the Kansas pro-slavery militia. He set John Jr. free (Jason had already been released), formed a new militia of free-state settlers, and used the United States army to keep the peace.

Osawatomie Brown, as John, Sr. was now known, felt stifled by peace. Raiders who had ridden with him returned to their farms, and those who had no farms were captured, or like himself, doomed to desolation and inactivity. John Jr. and Jason gathered up their small families and returned to Ohio. Finally Brown decided to give up Kansas and go home. Friends who had fought at Osawatomie or followed him in the saddle patted the old warrior on the back and promised to fight with him again should he decide to come back. Some of them did and would give their lives in the valley of the Potomac.

The Pottawatomie murders were always on John Brown's mind, not with regret, but because they were a stain upon the public conscience. After the Battle of Black Jack and the fight at Osawatomie he felt vindicated but uncertain of what people thought back East. He had other plans, secret plans, and to live out those plans he needed money—thousands of dollars to raise, equip, and train an army to topple slavery. Kansas was a proving ground and it gave him confidence. Now he needed wealthy backers, and if men were willing to invest their wealth to make Kansas free, maybe they would invest a little more to end slavery. He knew the men who held the purse strings, but he needed credibility to get their support.

Worn by exposure and shaken by chills, John Brown rode to Lawrence on September 14, 1856, to say good-bye to Dr. Robinson. The free-state leader asked him to stay. He wanted a few of his enemies kidnapped and thought Brown the perfect man to do it. Brown rejected the offer, and gave reasons why he had to go home. He asked Robinson for a letter recognizing his service to the free-state cause. The doctor complied by writing that Captain John Brown had earned his "sincere gratification" and had merited the "highest praise" from "every patriot." History would give his name a "proud place on her pages" for his heroism in "the cause of God and humanity."

Brown read the letter carefully and then asked for another, worded a little differently. Robinson picked up his pen and wrote the following:[31]

Lawrence, Sept. 14, 1856

To the Settlers of Kansas,— If possible, please render Captain John Brown all the assistance he may require in defending Kansas from invaders and outlaws, and you will confer a favor upon your co-laborer and fellow-citizen.

C. Robinson.

Brown tucked the letters into his leather pouch. They were far more valuable than the hundred dollars he needed to get home.

Malaria, Brown's lifelong nemesis, struck as he started east. He stopped at Tabor, Iowa, and stored his guns in the basement of Reverend John Todd. When his health improved, he continued east, stopping at the office of the National Kansas

Committee in Chicago. Horace White, the Committee's assistant secretary, greeted Brown and studied the letters written by Robinson. He took Brown to a tailor, fitted him out in a new suit of clothes, and gave him enough money for a comfortable trip home.[32]

During their meeting, White mentioned that two hundred Sharps rifles had just arrived from the Massachusetts Kansas Committee, and he asked Brown how they should be used. Without hesitation, Brown suggested to the committee's vice president, General J. D. Webster, that the "immediate introduction of the supplies [to Kansas] is not of much consequence compared to the danger of *losing* them."[33] Brown offered Reverend Todd's basement in Tabor as the safest place to store the rifles. He added that when he returned in the spring, he would evaluate conditions in Kansas and recommend the best way to distribute them. With Brown's excellent credentials from Robinson, the committee agreed to his proposal. But the guns were already on their way across Iowa, escorted coincidentally by Salmon and Watson Brown. They had come west to kill Reverend Martin White, Frederick's murderer, and before leaving New York, they had stopped at Peterboro and obtained enough cash from Gerrit Smith to act out their revenge. Brown wired Owen at Tabor to hold the guns until he arrived. A few days later he joined his sons and stored what later became his personal Harpers Ferry arsenal in Reverend Todd's home. One wayward spark, touching any of the many kegs of gunpowder stored in Todd's basement, could have blown up half of the town of Tabor.[34]

Brown's stopover in Chicago had netted more than guns. There he had met Reverend Theodore Parker, an influential Boston abolitionist. Parker suggested that if Brown needed money to fight slavery in Kansas, he should go to the offices of the Massachusetts Kansas Committee and talk with Franklin Sanborn, the committee's secretary. Sanborn could open doors and lead him to the men with the deep pockets. Parker gave Brown a letter of introduction, but by the time Brown reached Boston, Parker was already there.[35]

On the way east, Brown stopped in Columbus, Ohio, and called upon Governor Salmon P. Chase. The meeting was a dry run before he reached the Smith mansion in Peterboro. The governor read Robinson's letters and commended Brown warmly for his services. On a piece of personal stationery he scribbled an endorsement to go with Robinson's letters, referring to Captain John Brown as "a highly reputable citizen of this State" and "as a gentleman every way worthy of entire confidence...."[36] Chase had probably never heard of the bankrupt speculator, or the midnight rider who pulled citizens from their beds and split open their heads on the banks of the Pottawatomie. John Brown was a common name. The interview ended when Chase dipped into his wallet and squeezed twenty-five dollars into the palm of Brown's gnarled hand.[37]

Now it was time to see Gerrit Smith.

4
The Secret Six

John Brown stopped at Peterboro on his way to Boston. He now had a reputation as a freedom fighter, and an arsenal hidden in the cellar of Reverend Todd's home. The guns and ammunition were not his, but he meant to keep them. A little cash jingled in his pocket, but to pursue his plan he needed more money—much more.

On Dec. 30, 1856, Gerrit Smith received the old warrior warmly, seated him in front of the huge hearth in the parlor, and listened intently to Brown's account of self-sacrifice. For several hours Brown described conditions in Kansas, how his son's families had been burned out and driven from their shelters and how Missourians had captured John Jr. and Jason and dragged them in chains across the hot prairie. He spoke of the ravaging of Osawatomie, and finally of Frederick's murder by the smoking gun of a pro-slavery preacher. Smith, capable of great emotion, wept tears and gave the gaunt man from "Bleeding Kansas" money for his Boston expenses. More importantly, he read Brown's packet of neatly folded letters and wrote:[1]

> Captain John Brown,—You did not need to show me letters...to let me know who you are. I have known you many years, and have highly esteemed you as long as I have known you. I know your unshrinkable bravery, your self-sacrificing benevolence, your devotion to the cause of freedom, and have long known them. May heaven preserve your life and health, and prosper your noble purposes!
>
> Gerrit Smith

Brown had not visited his wife and younger children for more than seventeen months, but he was so anxious to get to Boston he postponed going home. Franklin Sanborn met the old gentleman enthusiastically and with him, hurried to see Dr.

FRANKLIN B. SANBORN
(Kansas State Historical Society, Topeka)

Howe and Theodore Parker. During the next few days, Brown met George Luther Stearns, Amos A. Lawrence, Judge Thomas Russell, Wendell Phillips and William Lloyd Garrison, all eminent abolitionists connected with the Massachusetts Kansas Committee. Shortly thereafter he met Thomas Wentworth Higginson, an outspoken disunionist. By listening carefully, he discovered that his new friends could agree on the problem—slavery—but not on the solution. He had met Howe, Parker, and Lawrence briefly in the past, but the others were new faces with a common relationship. They all knew Gerrit Smith and depended, at times, upon his support and his wealth.

When Smith sent Brown to see Sanborn, he probably knew that the young, educated idealist would instantly admire and respect the old warrior. Emotionally,

Smith and Sanborn were much alike, but in January, 1857, the Peterboro land baron was fifty-nine, whereas Sanborn was a young schoolteacher fresh out of Harvard. Sanborn admired Smith for his great philanthropy, and Theodore Parker for his outspoken, often militant stand against slavery. Influenced by both, Sanborn joined the Middlesex County Kansas Committee and traveled to the Territory to investigate how funds were being spent. His trip west exposed him to the conflict and to the many dangers faced by families who lived a few days' ride by horseback from the Kansas-Missouri border. Sanborn did not have the courage or the tenacity of Kansas settlers. Still, he envied the determination and leadership abilities of free-state men like Charles Robinson, Jim Lane and John Brown, whose exploits made headline news in the Eastern press. When Sanborn returned, George Luther Stearns offered him the position of secretary of the Massachusetts Kansas Committee, and Parker suggested he take it. Sanborn, who considered himself a better administrator than fighter, accepted the post. By doing so, he irretrievably connected himself with John Brown.[2]

Born on August 10, 1810, Theodore Parker, the son of a Massachusetts farmer, entered Harvard Divinity School at the age of twenty-four—a place he later described as one great "embalming institution." As pastor of the Twenty-eighth Congregational Society in Boston, he preached for several years to mixed audiences in the huge downtown Music Hall. A man of massive intelligence and a voracious reader, Parker began to question conventional Unitarian philosophy, broke with the church, and became a leading transcendentalist with a huge following. Drawn into the antislavery movement by Howe, abolitionism gradually dominated his time and energy. By 1846 he had become an outspoken leader, declaring that "all the great charters of humanity are writ in blood and must continue to be for some centuries." Parker built his abolitionist foundation on the concept of Higher Law, which coincided exactly with Brown's view that God's law superseded civil law in all matters, and especially on those pertaining to slavery. He denounced the Fugitive Slave Act, joined the Boston Vigilance Committee, and after returning from Chicago, he considered John Brown a man of action and a man for the times.[3]

Parker had met Howe in Rome in 1843 at a time when the doctor was ending his involvement in the Greek revolution and turning his attention to reform. Howe, born in 1801, had just married twenty-four year old Julia Ward, an intellectually gifted woman of strong convictions who exerted considerable influence over her husband. Parker's abomination of slavery, combined with the doctor's own experiences in Greece, drew him into the anti-slavery movement soon after he returned to the States. In 1846 he ran for public office as a Conscience Whig but lost. Two years later he supported the Free Soil Party. He actively participated in escorting dozens of runaway slaves through Boston, sending them to Canada or to small farms like those provided by Gerrit Smith.

In 1850, as John Brown circulated through Springfield organizing his league of black Gileadites, Howe stumped for arch-abolitionist Charles Sumner's election to the United States Senate. When the Fugitive Slave Act passed, he helped Parker and others form the Boston Vigilance Committee. By now, he had accepted Parker's Higher Law principles, and with financial help from men like Stearns, he created the powerful Massachusetts Kansas Committee. In July, 1856, he went with Eli Thayer

SAMUEL GRIDLEY HOWE
(Library of Congress)

to Buffalo, New York, to help form a National Kansas Committee with auxiliaries in every state, county and town. He heard Gerrit Smith submit a series of militant resolutions and listened to the debate that followed. After that, he went to Kansas and berated Jim Lane for instigating violence. The Greek revolutionary could not bring himself to endorse bloodshed as a means of resisting unjust laws—at least, not yet.[4]

By 1856, forty-eight-year-old George Luther Stearns had risen from a family of modest means to become a wealthy and influential businessman. Stearns borrowed large sums of money, but unlike Brown, he made timely investments and soon prospered. Like Smith, he joined the Liberty Party, and like Howe, he financially backed Sumner's senatorial campaign.

GEORGE LUTHER STERNS
(Library of Congress)

After building a mansion in Medford, Massachusetts, Stearns contributed large sums of money to various charities without any clear object in mind. But when the Fugitive Slave Act passed in 1850, he purchased his first revolver and vowed that no runaway "would be taken from his premises." As a Conscience Whig, he met Howe, and during a convention in Worcester, he met Thomas Wentworth Higginson. When the small Whig constituency failed to grow politically, he attached himself to the Liberty Party. The Fugitive Slave Act brought Parker, Howe, Higginson and Stearns together.

When in 1855 South Carolinian Preston Brooks caned Charles Sumner on the floor of the Senate, Stearns declared that the act would "make a million abolitionists," and he vowed to devote "his life and fortune to the cause." Two weeks later he joined the Massachusetts Kansas Committee, and the following year replaced Howe as its chairman.

Stearns and Howe were close friends and often debated Parker's concept of Higher Law. The Medford philanthropist believed in "Christian living," and shared Howe's theories on reform. Stearns had great respect for Parker, but like Howe, he was not ready to adopt violence or slave insurrection. With Gerrit Smith he shared a deep compassion for his fellow man and could be moved to feelings of great empathy. Unlike Howe and Sanborn, Stearns, who was now chairman of the Massachusetts Kansas Committee, had not been to the Territory. When he met the gaunt old guerrilla fresh from the blood-stained prairie who spoke of God's fight to protect freedom, he saw the embodiment of an ultimate Christian. Sanborn, who desperately wanted to give Brown help but had no money himself, convinced Stearns that Captain Brown was a good investment and would give his life and those of his sons to keep Kansas free. Brown probably knew that the Sharps rifles stored in Todd's Tabor basement had been donated by Stearns, and besides money to carry his campaign into Virginia, he wanted those guns.[5]

Of the six men who would ultimately bond together to finance the balance of John Brown's life, no one took a more militant stand than thirty-three year old Thomas Wentworth Higginson, who had entered Harvard at the age of thirteen. He graduated Phi Beta Kappa and had no idea what to do with his life. At his family's urging, he entered Harvard Divinity School in 1844 but found Unitarian theology "overbearing" and inconsistent with his own personal philosophy. He would have agreed with Parker's description of the school as "a great embalming institution." Higginson left his studies after one year, his career still undecided. But there was something about Parker's radical ideas of theology that appealed to him, so he returned to school resolved to become "a leader of men." In 1847, he graduated at the top of his class at Harvard Divinity School and gave the graduation address, speaking on "The Clergy and Reform." Parker sat in the audience, astounded by the young man who had captured the essence of his own thoughts. He met with Higginson after the ceremonies, and the two men formed a lasting friendship that hurled both of them into the midst of John Brown's trip to Boston.[6]

Higginson, whose Higher Law sermons rattled conservative Unitarians, finally settled in Worcester where Parker had already converted the congregation. Then in 1854 Higginson took the law into his own hands by leading an assault on Boston's jail to free Anthony Burns, a captured fugitive being returned to his master. Parker and Howe joined a mob of protesters in the street. But they were less inclined than Higginson to batter down the doors of civil law and stood aside, shocked by their colleague's violence. Unlike his friends, Higginson thereafter preached disunion as the only solution to the slave problem. When he began to understand the mind of John Brown, he all but shunned his friends with impatience for their lack of resolve in turning the old man loose with guns and money.[7]

Higginson, too, had been to the Territories in the summer of 1856. He had spoken to angry settlers, seen the destruction in Lawrence, and listened to accounts about defenders of freedom like Captain Brown. On November 1, he wrote to Smith, declaring that men were better prepared for revolution than ever. Among Kansas settlers he detected an absence of "that spirit of blind, superstitious loyalty to the U.S. government which I feared to find. On the contrary, the people of Kansas are just as ready to fight the U.S. government as the Missourians, so far as feeling is concerned." Higginson suggested that private companies of volunteers be organized and kept ready to answer any call. He urged Smith to help in making the enterprise a success by supporting it with cash.[8]

John Brown had similar thoughts and asked for $30,000.00 to equip a company of one hundred mounted rangers for service in Kansas and Missouri. The sum seemed small compared to the million dollars allocated in the original budgets of the various Kansas Committees. Sanborn was optimistic. He paraded Brown before the Massachusetts State Legislature, the Massachusetts Kansas Committee, and the National Kansas Committee. Higginson invited Brown to speak at a disunion convention in Worcester, speculating that additional funds could be collected from the committee's members.

At first, the meetings and discussions went well. Brown elaborated on the conditions in Kansas and used his family's misfortunes to make his case. He evoked sympathy by waving the chains that had manacled John Jr. and described the beatings that had knocked him senseless. With exciting adjectives, he embellished the battle at Black Jack, the defense of Osawatomie, the burning of Lawrence, and the murder of Frederick. Afterward, nobody asked him about the Pottawatomie killings. The National Kansas Committee appropriated five thousand dollars to "Captain John Brown in any defensive measures that may become necessary [to protect Kansas settlers], and...he is hereby authorized to draw upon the treasurer for the sum of five hundred dollars." Brown did not want conditions like "defensive measures" attached to the money, but he would save that issue until later. The National Kansas Committee also returned the two hundred rifles stored at Tabor to Stearns, chairman of the Massachusetts Committee, who in turn asked that they be given to Brown. Although the committee would give him no more money, they furnished enough clothes and equipment for fifty of the captain's so-called rangers.[9]

Before speaking to the Massachusetts legislature, Brown made a hurried trip to Peterboro. Gerrit Smith, who gave money to many causes, was still a businessman who expected to be paid for land sold, including John Brown's North Elba farm. Smith would carry the note and help the captain with expenses, but the farm would not be donated. Despite his annual income of over $60,000.00 a year, Smith anticipated another bout of tight money and turned conservative. In February, Brown was back in Boston looking for funds to pay for the farm. Sanborn suggested that he see Amos Lawrence, who with some reluctance agreed to poll his friends for subscriptions. Brown wanted $1,000.00, enough to buy the farm and support his family when he returned to Kansas. By summer, Lawrence and Stearns had raised the money, over half of it their own, and turned it over to Sanborn to cover Brown's debts.[10]

On February 17 the Massachusetts legislature listened skeptically to testimony from Brown and others familiar with Kansas affairs. With help from Brown, Sanborn hoped to raise $100,000.00 for his committee, a share of which would go to the captain. Since Brown had come east, John Geary had become governor of Kansas, the border had grown quiet. The legislature was aware of this and wondered why Brown needed so much money to defend peaceful Kansas settlers. Brown discredited Geary's pacification claims as a passing phenomenon and replied to questions by saying, "Whenever we heard last year that the people of the North were doing anything for us, we were encouraged and strengthened to keep up the contest. At present there is not much danger of an invasion from Missouri. God protects us in winter; but when the grass gets high enough to feed the horses of the Border Ruffians we may have trouble, and should be prepared for the worst." Brown concluded his remarks by declaring that Geary and the "Federal Government is wholly on the side of slavery."

When the chairman asked what kind of emigrants Kansas needed, Brown replied, curiously omitting any reference to slavery: "We want good men, industrious men, men who respect themselves; who act only from the dictates of conscience; men who fear God too much to fear anything human." Despite Brown's predictions of violence, the Massachusetts legislature appropriated not a penny for Kansas or for Captain Brown. Sanborn was stunned.[11]

Brown did slightly better at Higginson's disunion convention. He obtained $500.00 in arms, including a small cannon, but what he needed was cash. Sanborn suggested he go on a lecture circuit, and for more than a month Brown traveled throughout New England, Pennsylvania and New York. He spoke to small groups, sipped tea with wealthy women, flourished John Jr.'s chains, and passed the hat. When Brown tallied his collections, he had a few hundred dollars and a carpetbag full of pledges.[12]

Still optimistic, Brown met Charles Blair, a blacksmith who had attended his lecture in Collinsville, Connecticut. Blair admired a two-edged dirk that Brown flourished in a local drug store and commented that he could make about a thousand, mounted on poles, for a dollar a piece. Brown placed an order, claiming they "would be a capital weapon of defense for the settlers of Kansas to keep in their cabins...against any sudden attack that might be made on them." Kansas settlers had no use for such weapons, but Brown was thinking ahead to the slaves of Virginia who knew nothing of firearms.[13]

On one of his trips to New York, Brown met Hugh Forbes, a suave adventurer who called himself a colonel and claimed to have served under Garibaldi in the Italian revolution. As a bankrupt English silk merchant from Siena, Forbes came to New York in 1855 and scraped out a living by translating for the *Tribune*, doing odd jobs, and giving fencing lessons. Impressed by the guerrilla fighter, Brown believed he had found in Forbes the perfect expert to drill his men for the coming invasion of Virginia. For a man who usually kept his own counsel, Brown made the mistake of disclosing his hidden plan to an unstable opportunist whom he barely knew. Forbes envisioned rich opportunities for himself by joining Brown's revolution against slavery. He gullibly accepted the captain's assertion that commitments of large sums had been made by influential backers. In desperate need of funds himself, he flimflammed his way into Brown's shallow pockets. In a matter of days, he joined the plot for a salary of one hundred dollars a month, a sum which Brown could hardly afford. He agreed to write a manual on guerrilla warfare and train the captain's company. Since Brown planned to leave for Kansas, he gave Forbes authority to draw his salary from funds in Hartford, and the Englishman immediately withdrew the full amount, emptying the account. By now, drillmaster Forbes even knew the names of Brown's secret backers and was convinced they would make him rich.[14]

Brown said good-bye to Forbes and returned to Boston to collect his war chest. Stearns had consolidated all his available cash and authorized Brown to draw up to $7,000.00. Other cash, pledges, supplies, rifles, revolvers, and ammunition brought the total to about $23,000.00. Brown planned to stop in Ohio, Chicago, and small towns on the route to Kansas and use his speaking talents to pocket a little more. He picked up Owen at North Elba and in mid-May started west, commenting militantly "with Irons in rather than *uppon* our hands."[15]

On his way to Kansas, John Brown assumed the alias of Nelson Hawkins, partly to shield his identity and partly because it enhanced his mystique. Suffering from malaria, he took his time reaching Tabor. Letters he received from Kansas cohorts convinced him that Governor Geary had indeed stemmed bloodshed and speedily brought all of the troublemakers to justice. This was gloomy news since most of his promised money depended upon active operations in *defense* of the free-soil cause.

When Brown learned that Gerrit Smith had come to Chicago to encourage Midwest lawmakers to fight the fugitive slave law, the captain was nearly out of money. The $600.00 paid to Forbes and the $550.00 paid to Blair for pikes had stripped him of cash and left him with nothing but a carpetbag filled with uncollectible pledges. He had planned to raise money as he drifted west, but another malaria had disabled him for weeks. He found Smith furious over President Buchanan's apparent support of a pro-slavery government in Kansas. There is no record of the discussion between the two men, but shortly after Brown left, Smith wrote Thaddeus Hyatt, "We must not shrink from fighting for Liberty—and if Federal troops fight against her, we must fight against them." Evidently, Brown had reestablished his worth as a fighter because Smith gave his "old friend" $350.00 for his operations and another $110.00 to pay off another North Elba debt.[16]

On August 7, Brown arrived in Tabor. He sifted through a small pile of waiting mail, tore each envelope open and glumly cast them aside. There was no money from his friends back East, only a small draft of $110.00 from Edmund B. Whitman, the Lawrence agent for the Massachusetts Kansas Committee. Desperate, and still weakened by fever, Brown scribbled a letter to Stearns (who had pledged but not paid $7,000.00) pleading for "from Five Hundred to One Thousand Dollars for secret service & no questions asked." Brown wrote that "interesting times" were expected in Kansas, but he had been unable to travel beyond Tabor and had little knowledge of what was happening in the territory.

Two days later Forbes arrived demanding more money. On his way west he had stopped in Chicago and tapped Gerrit Smith for $150.00, claiming the money was needed to print his manual. Brown shared his remaining cash with Forbes, but this did not satisfy the Englishman. For several days the two men argued over money, strategy, tactics, and command responsibility. Forbes considered himself superior to Brown as a military commander and hoped to lead the campaign. He believed Brown, "with his bigoted mind and limited instruction," incapable of leading a large body of guerrillas, adding that Brown "might have been useful in some capacity" if he discarded the habit of deluding himself. Forbes also complained that he had come to Iowa to train an army and the only soldier present was Owen Brown, who had a crippled right arm.[17]

THEODORE PARKER
(Library of Congress)

Brown was still sick, unsure about Kansas, and by September so short of funds he was living off the generosity of his Tabor friends. He had nothing to report to his Eastern backers and had stopped writing, except to beg money from Sanborn. Militants like Higginson wanted to know why Brown had not struck a blow. Sanborn, who had doubts himself, defended the old warrior by trying to explain his circumstances. "He is ready for a revolution as any other man, and is now on the borders of Kansas, safe from arrest but prepared for action, but he needs money for his present expenses, and active support." He exhorted Higginson, "If you can do anything for Brown now, in God's name do it, and the ill result of the new policy in Kansas may be prevented." But Higginson, like every other man in mid-1857 England, had no money to send. Even Stearns reneged on his pledge of $7,000.00.[18]

THOMAS WENTWORTH HIGGINSON
(U.S. Army Military History Institute)

Forbes tired of waiting for money. After he milked Brown for his last sixty dollars he became surly, suspecting the captain of attempting to ease him out of the scheme. Each day he became more disruptive, accusing Stearns and Howe of maliciously and deliberately attempting to wrong him personally, while starving "by slow torture" his wife and children. As days passed, he scoffed at Brown's so-called "well-matured plan." Where were the men to train? In late October, Brown received $250.00 and started to Kansas to find recruits. He shared part of the money with Forbes, who then mysteriously disappeared and drifted back east. For Brown, Forbes' departure was good riddance.[19]

Brown succeeded in gathering nine recruits, some of whom would later follow him into Virginia. But in the fall of 1857, a good reason to invade Kansas never presented itself. In December he collected all the guns and supplies and set out for Ohio to establish a training school, but harsh weather and no money forced him to stop at Springdale, Iowa. Brown left his men behind to drill under Aaron Dwight Stevens, an army deserter with military experience, and returned east to recruit black volunteers.

Before disclosing his whereabouts to his backers, he hid for a month in Frederick Douglass' home in Rochester, New York, staying mostly to himself while he perfected his Virginia plan. In many ways, Brown needed Douglass almost as badly as he needed money. Blacks trusted Douglass, and Brown needed blacks to fill the ranks of his army. Douglass agreed to help and eventually put Brown in touch with Negro leaders in the Northeast and Canada. Brown also needed to have Douglass make inquiries into Forbes' activities. The disgruntled drillmaster had stopped to beg a few dollars from the black abolitionist before stopping at Peterboro to put the squeeze on Smith.[20]

While Douglass rallied black support and looked into Forbes' affairs, Brown created a somewhat remarkable document titled: "Provisional Constitution and Ordinances for the People of the United States." The so-called "Constitution" established a separate government composed of himself, his men, and all who joined him. The new order would operate in the mountains of the South until the federal government abolished slavery. In essence, John Brown's pen had discarded temporarily the United States Constitution and replaced it with a Higher Law provisional document with himself as its commander-in-chief. To Douglass, Brown's treasonable constitution was no more radical than the plan he had once outlined in his Springfield dining room when he opened a map and traced his bony finger southward, saying, "These mountains are the basis of my plan. God has given the strength of the hills to freedom; they were placed here for the emancipation of the Negro race."[21]

While Brown refined the Provisional Constitution, Douglass learned that Forbes had tried to blackmail Sanborn, Howe and Stearns and had threatened to disclose the plot to the federal government.[22] Brown immediately wrote his backers, and announced that he was now perfecting "BY FAR the most important undertaking of my whole life," and that he needed five hundred to eight hundred dollars in the next sixty days to "perfect his arrangements for carrying out an important measure in which the world has a deep interest, as well as Kansas...." Stearns asked him to come to Boston, but Brown declined under the pretense of keeping his whereabouts unknown and suggested they all meet in Peterboro.[23]

Because of Brown's revelations to Forbes, Stearns questioned the captain's competence. Higginson had lost interest because Brown had gone to Kansas and failed to create a disruption. No one came to Brown's meeting in Peterboro but Sanborn, who used the trip as an excuse to see Edwin Morton, an old Harvard chum who lived with the Smiths and tutored their children.

Brown had another motive in calling for the meeting in the Smith mansion. He knew that his Bostonian friends had become critical of his relationship with Forbes. Through Frederick Douglass, however, he was equally aware that Smith had not changed his position on ending slavery even if it meant fighting federal troops. With Smith's wealth and generosity, Brown hoped to hold onto one important source of funds even if his Boston backers deserted him. He also felt certain that if Smith supported him the others would. Brown was disappointed when only Sanborn agreed to attended the meeting.[24]

In the hospitable atmosphere of the Peterboro mansion, Brown slowly and deliberately revealed his plan to Smith. When Sanborn arrived four days later, Brown felt certain of Smith's support. The men retired to a cozy third floor bedroom and sat around a table as Brown paced the floor and read excerpts from his Provisional Constitution. He explained in detail his methods of organization and fortification, the raising of troops, the tactics and timing. His men would live off the land—land made wealthy by the work of slaves, land to which slaves were entitled. He argued that the time had passed for settling the slave issue through politics or other peaceful means. The black man's only recourse rested with God and a massive slave uprising that would spill the blood of slaveholders. He would incite the insurrection by a forced march through Virginia with a guerrilla force he was now raising. Even if the insurrection failed, Brown assured his listeners that the attempt would unify Northern hatred of slavery and provoke a crisis, perhaps even a civil war. Then the black man's chains would be broken on the battlefield. During this meeting, there is no evidence that he mentioned his plan to attack the United States Armory at Harpers Ferry. He needed, however, eight hundred dollars—a small sum—to put his plan in motion. When asked how he expected to accomplish so much with so little, Brown replied with a text of Scripture: "If God be for us, who can be against us?"[25]

On February 23 the discussions continued. Sanborn slowly saw that he must either convince the men in Boston to stand by Brown or the old warrior would "dash himself alone against the fortress he was determined to assault."[26] Sanborn realized that only a strong commitment from Smith would hold Stearns, Higginson and the others together. He left Brown with Morton and strolled through the snow-covered fields with Smith at his side. They talked of Brown's noble plan, and wondered whether it was madness or an act of divine brilliance. As Smith once had said: "Much as I abhor war, I nevertheless believe, that there are instances when the shedding of blood is unavoidable." Now Captain Brown of Osawatomie was mobilizing a force to do it all himself, and Smith felt bound by personal conviction to "go all lengths" to support him.[27]

"You see how it is," Smith said to Sanborn, "our dear friend has made up his mind to this course, and cannot be turned from it. We cannot give him up to die alone; we must support him. I will raise so many hundred dollars for him; you must lay the case before your friends in Massachusetts and perhaps they will do the same. I see no other way."[28]

On February 20, 1858, Brown wrote to his son, John Jr., "I am most happy to tell you [that Gerrit Smith and his wife] are ready to go in for a share in the whole trade. I will say in the language of another in regard to this most encouraging fact, 'My soul doth magnify the Lord'. I seem to be almost marvelously helped; and to His name be praise!" Four days later he passed the good news to his wife and family.[29] Smith's approval of Brown's plan carried substantial weight, giving not only a guarantee of financial support, but moral standing as well. Brown had reason to celebrate.

Sanborn, also pleased with Smith's commitment, agreed to promote Brown's proposal among Stearns, Howe, Parker and Higginson and organize a meeting with the captain as soon as possible. On March 4, 1858, Brown checked into Boston's

American House on Hanover Street and for four days discussed minute details of his grand scheme. He carefully avoided mentioning Harpers Ferry as the target of his first attack. Like Smith, the listeners accepted the mountains of Virginia as the battleground. They all knew that Brown thought of himself as an agent appointed by God to punish sinful men and bring an end to slavery, but they worried about Brown's indiscreet disclosures to Forbes and wondered how many other people knew of the plan. Men like Howe, who still remembered the Greek Revolution, doubted the soundness of Brown's invasion. But after four days of debate, Higginson, Stearns, Howe and Parker agreed that all peaceful alternatives had failed and only revolution was left. Sanborn summarized the consensus by saying, "Without accepting [all of] Brown's plans as reasonable, we were prepared to second them merely because they were his." Higginson and Parker doubted if the old warrior with the "thin, worn, resolute face" would succeed, but they were willing to let him try, convinced that an invasion of Southern soil would ignite a powder keg that might yet explode into civil war.[30]

Before Brown departed from Boston to recruit his black army, Sanborn informed him that a secret committee of six, including Gerrit Smith, had been formed to raise $1,000.00. Smith, who took Brown's plans as seriously as Brown himself, was ecstatic and wrote his Ohio friend Joshua Giddings, "The slave will be delivered by the shedding of blood—and the signs are multiplying that his deliverance is at hand."[31]

Brown intended to launch his attack in early May, 1858. In March he traveled through Philadelphia, New York, and Syracuse rallying support. Then in April he went into Canada, where forty thousand blacks lived, and tried to raise a hundred men. He moved on to Chatham, Ontario, and held a convention, hoping that Frederick Douglass, Harriet Tubman, and members of the Secret Six would help attract support. But only thirty-four blacks and twelve whites dignified the meeting with their curiosity. Midway through the convention, Brown received a summons from Sanborn to drop everything and come to Boston. Forbes had just revealed "the plan" to important members of Congress and had driven the little band of six conspirators into a panic.[32]

Smith reacted in step with Howe and Stearns. He wrote Higginson: "It seems to me that in these circumstances Brown must go no further, and so I write him. I never was convinced of the wisdom of his scheme. But as things now stand, it seems to me it would be madness to attempt to execute it. Colonel Forbes would make such an attempt a certain and most disastrous failure."[33]

Unlike Smith, Higginson manifested no signs of timidity and complained to Parker that he regarded "any postponement as simply abandoning the project; for if we give it up now, at the command or threat of H. F. [Hugh Forbes], it will be the same next year. The only way is to circumvent the man somehow....When the thing is well started, who cares what he says?"[34]

Stearns seemed to care, at least at the moment. On May 14 he wrote to Brown in Canada that "in consequence" of Forbes' revelations to Senator William H. Seward and others, he was not to use the rifles placed in his custody by the Massachusetts Kansas Committee "for any other purpose, and to hold them subject to my order as chairman of said committee."[35]

Gerrit Smith, who seldom went to Boston, checked into the Revere House on May 24 and attended a meeting of the Secret Six. It was the first time he had met with his associates as a group, and they named him chairman of the meeting. Higginson boycotted the session because he knew that Parker, Howe, Stearns and Sanborn had agreed to postpone the venture into Virginia for at least a year. They reasoned that if Brown went back to Kansas, it would discredit Forbes' allegations, and important senators like Henry Wilson and William H. Seward would regard the information as nonsense. Smith, who had been struggling to resolve his own ambivalence on Brown's conspiratorial intentions, agreed with the compromise. The meeting ended with several important resolutions. They would send Brown back to Kansas, and to shield themselves from the possibility of a future investigation, they asked him to not share the details of his plans with them. When he returned in the fall, the committee promised to give him at least $2,000.00, much of which would come from Gerrit Smith, with no questions asked. In addition, Brown would retain possession of the Sharps rifles as Stearn's agent. The old warrior accepted the terms dolefully and headed back to Kansas. Before leaving, he had a conversation with Higginson and expressed his profound disgust at the committee's lack of courage. "G S he knew to be a timid man," he said. But "G S" had the money.[36]

After the Secret Six adjourned, Smith delivered the principal address at the annual meeting of the American Peace Society. Referring to Kansas, he voiced a somewhat incongruous doctrine to many of his listeners: "I add that the irregular but righteous government which such an emergency calls into being is worthy to be sustained by good men the earth over—by their prayers, their contributions of food, clothing, money, and if need be, of 'Sharp's rifles' also." George C. Beckwith, president of the Peace Society, took exception to Smith's use of rifles, and critics complained that the speech lacked unity and logical continuity of thought. At the time, Smith was still restructuring his position on Brown's project and had not made up his mind. Nonetheless, the American Peace Society printed 280,000 copies of Smith's controversial address.[37]

Brown returned to Kansas intent upon accomplishing three objectives: first, he would create enough publicity to refute Forbes' accusations; then, he would gather a nucleus of men for his little army; and finally, he would secure the weapons needed for his Virginia campaign. He recruited a small force of hardened raiders and with another border chieftain, James Montgomery, led raids on pro-slavery strongholds. News of his activities drifted into Eastern newspapers, elating his backers.

During the summer, Gerrit Smith redefined his own attitude towards Brown. "I have great faith in the wisdom, integrity, and bravery of Captain Brown," he wrote Sanborn. "For several years I have frequently given him money towards sustaining him in his conquests with the slave-power. Whenever he shall embark in another of these contests I shall again stand ready to help him; and I will begin with giving him a hundred dollars. I do not wish to know Captain Brown's plans. I hope he will keep them to himself."[38]

John Brown built a fort on the Kansas-Missouri border and waited for an opportunity to kidnap a few slaves and bring them north to freedom. His opportunity came late in the fall. Dividing his force into two companies, one under himself and the other under Aaron Dwight Stevens, he crossed into Missouri, raided two plantations, and collected eleven slaves. Unfortunately, Stevens shot David Cruise, one of the farmers, and added a sixth murder to Brown's escapades in Kansas. The governor of Missouri offered $3,000.00 for Brown's capture; President James Buchanan added another $250.00.[39] When Gerrit Smith read of the raid, he wrote his wife an excited letter, "Do you hear the news from Kansas? Our dear John Brown is invading Kansas and pursuing the policy which he intended to pursue elsewhere."[40]

With enormous hardship, Brown and his caravan of blacks crossed the fierce windy plains of Kansas, Nebraska and Iowa in the dead of winter. They were chased by hundreds of armed men in posses out to pocket the big reward. Brown struggled eastward, rejected by former friends in towns like Tabor and Springdale who had heard of the murder of David Cruise. With help from a few sympathizers along the Underground Railroad, the caravan finally reached Detroit on March 12, 1859. Frederick Douglass met them at the train station and put the blacks on a ferry to Canada. For John Brown, the hegira had ended. Now he wanted his money.[41]

Sanborn knew the old warrior was coming east and informed the other members of the Secret Six that "Mr. Smith proposes to raise $1,000.00 for him," implying that the rest of the money must come from the Boston backers. Brown stopped at Cleveland, herded together his band of followers, and told them to find work until he called for them. Then he boarded a train for Peterboro. Once again, it was time to see Gerrit Smith.[42]

5
The Raid

On April 11, 1859, John Brown accompanied by Jeremiah G. Anderson stopped at Gerrit Smith's mansion for a four day visit.[1] The old warrior from the plains had grown a long silver beard, and all he needed to resemble an ancient oracle of the Lord was a matching white robe. To a small group gathered in Smith's spacious living room, Brown recounted his recent travails in Kansas with such eloquence that Smith and several of his guests were moved to tears. Edwin Morton remembered someone asking Brown if he had not better apply himself in another direction. He reminded him of his imminent peril, and stated that his life should not be sacrificed. Brown jumped to his feet, and swiftly replied that his life was unimportant if giving it would lead to the end of slavery. A little later, Gerrit Smith passed around a paper with his name at the top, pledging $400.00, to which the other guests added $35.00 more.[2]

Smith, who had changed his attitude many times toward the Kansas fighter, declared with emotional eloquence to his guests:

"If I were asked to point out—I will say it in his presence—to point out the man in this world I think most truly a Christian, I would point to John Brown. I was once doubtful in my own mind as to Captain Brown's course. I now approve it heartily, having given my mind to it more of late."[3]

Brown had not seen his family for a year. He now departed for North Elba, but his principal mission was to recruit his sons and the Thompson brothers, William and Dauphin. For more than two weeks he fought malarial fevers and violent headaches, and for a while doubted if he would ever recover. Early in May he felt strong enough to travel and departed for Concord, stopping briefly at Troy to buy provisions and supplies for his needy family.[4]

On his fifty-ninth birthday, May 9, 1859, Brown contacted Sanborn and asked if the young educator believed the Kansas diversion had "blinded Forbes." Sanborn replied it had. Brown said he would tolerate no more postponements and intimated that it was time for the Boston backers to make good on their promise. Sanborn, a man of small means, handed Brown $25.00 and the next day escorted the bearded raider and his bodyguard to Boston.[5]

Long before Brown reached Boston, Sanborn had been pressing both Smith and Stearns for the promised money. On May 16, while Brown waited for his war chest to fill, he nonetheless "urgently" tapped Gerrit Smith for additional funds. The Peterboro philanthropist wrote:

> My dear friend,—I have done what I could thus far for Kansas, and what I could to keep you at your Kansas work. Losses by endorsement and otherwise have brought me under heavy embarrassment the last two years, but I must, nevertheless, continue to do, in order to keep you at your Kansas work. I send you herewith my draft for two hundred dollars....My wife joins me in affectionate regard to you, dear John, whom we both hold in very high esteem.

Smith's reference to "Kansas work" was a concealment having nothing to do with work in Kansas. This letter would later turn up at Harpers Ferry and cause Smith great anxiety.[6]

When Brown reached Boston, his first reaction was disappointment. Parker was in Rome dying of consumption and could give no help. Howe condemned Brown's Missouri raid because he disapproved of shooting farmers and stealing horses. Higginson stayed away from Sanborn's meeting because he had lost interest, not in Brown, but in the frail resolve of the others. Only Stearns, Smith and Sanborn remained steadfast and by early June raised $2,000.00, much of it their own money. Sanborn, who tried to keep a record of monies received and disbursed, wrote that Smith had given Brown up to June, 1858, $750.00, while "Mr. Stearns in that year gave him more than a thousand." In a final tally, Sanborn said that over $3,800.00 had been contributed through efforts of the Secret Six for Brown's "Virginia enterprise." Sanborn, however, did not know of the private outpouring of funds from Smith to Brown in small installments of a few hundred dollars at a time.[7]

When Brown set out for Harpers Ferry in mid-June, he had $800.00 in cash in his pocket and the balance on its way. Before heading into Virginia with two of his sons, Owen and Oliver, and Jerry Anderson, he stopped at Collinsville to see Charles Blair about the pikes he had ordered in 1857. Blair barely recognized the old man behind the freshly trimmed beard. He agreed to finish the pikes but did not understand why Brown wanted them shipped to Chambersburg, Pennsylvania, instead of to Kansas. Brown, who now called himself Isaac Smith, had sent John Henry Kagi, another of his Kansas raiders, to Chambersburg, about forty miles north of Harpers Ferry. There a small building had been rented under the name of J. Smith and Sons to receive arms, ammunition, supplies and recruits as they arrived from distant locations.

On July 3, 1859, "Isaac Smith" ascended the road along Maryland Heights and with his little company of three studied the town of Harpers Ferry, the first target on Brown's agenda. The small, bustling, industrial town was situated on a rocky neck of land. It was surrounded on one side by the Potomac River and on the other by the

Shenandoah River, each spanned by bridges. Bolivar Heights rose sharply behind the town, leaving the Ferry in a hole surrounded on two of its three sides by water. Even an untrained military eye could observe that Harpers Ferry would be easy to attack but difficult to defend.

Five miles northeast of the Ferry, Brown rented the unoccupied Kennedy farm in Washington County, Maryland. The property contained a dilapidated home well back from the road and another small outbuilding large enough to store crates of military supplies. As Kagi sent each load of "freight" down the Boonsboro Pike from Chambersburg, Brown's boys piled it in a large storage area behind the kitchen on the ground floor of the Kennedy house. The second floor had two bedrooms, a living room and a dining room, but most of the recruits lived in the hot upper attic where they hid from nosy neighbors.[8]

From Chambersburg, Kagi sent messages to about a hundred men who, over a two year span of time, had committed themselves to Brown's project. They lived all over the country, from New York, Philadelphia and Boston to Kansas, Iowa and Ontario. Brown had no idea how many followers would respond to his summons, but he knew he must time his attack around their expected arrival. When only a few men dribbled slowly into Chambersburg, he postponed the raid, and time dragged from summer into fall.

In Peterboro, Gerrit Smith waited excitedly for news from Virginia. At times, he could think of nothing else. When anti-slavery leaders in Syracuse asked him to preside over the annual celebration of the Jerry [McHenry] Rescue, he shocked the membership by refusing. He then tartly berated all anti-slavery groups, political parties and religious denominations that still advocated moderation. Mr. Smith had suddenly become a Higher Law man, willing to break civil law if it differed from what he now called God's law.

John Brown stirred Smith's passions for equality and justice, or at least for the moment solidified his resolve. Smith, the former pacifist, replied to the committee: "No wonder is it that...intelligent black men in the States and Canada should see no hope for their race in the practice and policy of white men. No wonder they are brought to the conclusion that no resource is left to them but in God and insurrections. For insurrections then we may look any year, any month, any day. A terrible remedy for a terrible wrong! But come it must unless anticipated by repentance and the putting away of the terrible wrong." Smith admitted that insurrections might fail, but Southern communications would be destroyed, and across the land there would be widespread destruction. For their own security, slaveholders would give up the practice of bondage, Smith declared. After all, had not Thomas Jefferson predicted servile insurrection?[9]

Gerrit Smith's letter, which undoubtedly reflected some of the unrecorded conversations between himself and Brown, transcended normal curiosity and appeared in the New York *Tribune*. Had his readers known that his "dear friend, Captain Brown," was about to strike a blow at Harpers Ferry, they might have paid more attention. But most people who read the Jerry Rescue letter probably discarded it as one more effusion from the wealthy Peterboro landowner. In Washington, D.C., a Southern man responded anonymously and wrote Smith:

Sir, you are looked upon as a monster in human shape or by some perhaps as a Fiend from Hell sent upon the Earth to do his master's work in the most effectual manner he can, consistently with your own personal safety....I sincerely believe that there has been no such scheme of damnable villainy conceived since the Devil himself entered the Garden of Eden to bring ruin upon mankind by corrupting our first parents....You ought to be regarded rather as a principal than an accessory, and be dealt with accordingly.[10]

If Secretary of War John B. Floyd, a Virginian who hated abolitionists, had missed Smith's letter in the *Tribune*, he did not miss an unsigned letter sent to him by George Gill and several of Brown's Iowa friends who hoped to deter him, and perhaps save him, from attacking Harpers Ferry by warning the United States government. The letter reached Floyd while he was vacationing at Red Sweet Springs in Virginia. It stated that a "secret association, having for its objective the liberation of the slaves at the South by a general insurrection" was being led by "old John Brown, late of Kansas." After relating the details of Brown's preparations, the letter continued: "They will pass down through Pennsylvania and Maryland, and enter Virginia at Harpers Ferry. Brown left the North about three or four weeks ago, and will arm the negroes and strike the blow in a few weeks; so whatever is done must be done at once." The joint authors of the letter failed in their geography because they referred to "an armory in Maryland." Floyd knew of no armory in Maryland (Harpers Ferry was in Virginia), so he set the letter aside and relaxed to enjoy his vacation away from the problems of government.[11]

There is evidence that Smith remained in contact with Brown almost up to the time of the raid. Edwin Morton, who lived in the Peterboro mansion, said Smith "has his whole soul absorbed in this matter."[12] About this time, Brown needed another three hundred dollars to pay freight bills and buy provisions, and he wrote asking John Jr. to apply to "my Eastern or Western friends in regard to it....It is terribly humiliating to me to begin soliciting of friends again; but...I may not allow a feeling of delicacy to deter me from asking the little further aid I expect to need."[13] At the end of August, Smith sent another $100.00 to Brown.[14]

Brown's little one-horse covered wagon had been seen so often on the road between Chambersburg and the Kennedy farm that local sheriffs began to suspect "Isaac Smith" of transporting slaves to Pennsylvania. A nosy neighbor thought she had seen a black man in the Kennedy house once when she unexpectedly entered the kitchen. Brown had told a local farmer that he had come south to raise cattle, but after two months still had only one milk cow. Loquacious John Cook, one of Brown's men who had come to Harpers Ferry in 1858 to spy on the town, had talked liberally with too many people. As mid-October approached, Brown felt that he could wait no longer for more recruits. He had twenty-two men, among them five blacks and three of his sons, and they were all restless to the point of mutiny. Outside the circle of Brown's men, an estimated eighty people had heard of the projected invasion. Many others, such as Senators William H. Seward and Henry Wilson and Secretary of War Floyd, had some inkling that Brown was planning an incendiary move against the South.[15]

On October 16, 1859, Gerrit Smith and the Secret Six's patience was about to be rewarded with stunning effect. Shortly after dark, Brown gave the order, "Men, get on your arms; we will proceed to the Ferry."

It took only a few minutes for the men to bring the horse and wagon to the door and load it with pikes, fagots, a sledge-hammer and a crowbar. Three men remained at the Kennedy farm to distribute arms and supplies to slaves when they deserted their masters and joined the insurrection. Nineteen men with rifles slung under their grey shawls and revolvers shoved in their belts followed the captain through a misty drizzle as he nudged the mare down the hill to the Ferry. When he reached the covered railroad bridge spanning the Potomac, two men cut the telegraph wires to Baltimore and Washington and extinguished the lights. Kagi and Stevens advanced onto the bridge, captured the watchman, and the little company of raiders crossed into the Ferry. All was quiet. The men divided and took positions at strategic points: John Brown entered the United States Armory, Kagi occupied Hall's Rifle Works, Watson and Oliver Brown each took men and captured both bridges, and two of the raiders entered the two-story arsenal. Aaron Stevens took five men and circulated through the countryside, kidnapping important hostages like Colonel Lewis Washington, great-grandnephew of the first president, and recruited their bewildered slaves.

Shortly after midnight, a few people in the quiet town heard a muffled shot echo half-way down the covered B & O bridge spanning the Potomac River. Moments later the relief watchman came running into the Wager House, which doubled as the train station, with a gash across the top of his head. He was confused, and since there had been talk of a strike at the armory, he and the hotel clerk speculated that a few of the workmen had over-indulged in some bad whiskey and started the strike prematurely. A little later, the B & O from Wheeling rolled into town and the conductor refused to cross the bridge until he was certain it was safe. Three men started across the bridge to investigate, including the huge, portly baggage-master, Hayward Shepherd, who followed out of curiosity. Near the point on the bridge where the tracks formed a "Y" the two men bumped into Oliver Brown and Will Thompson who hollered "Halt! Don't move!" Both men turned and ran, and two shots whizzed over their heads. Brown's boys reloaded, looked down the covered way, and observed the dim outline of Shepherd's hulk formed against a backdrop of light. Sensing trouble, the baggage handler started to lumber down the tracks to safety, but a bullet struck his back and came out the left side of his chest. A few hours later, he died. The first fatality of Brown's invasion to liberate slaves was a free black man.[16]

With the body of the baggage-master lying on the platform outside the Wager House and daylight approaching, Brown's luck began to change. He had about forty hostages, more than he could handle. His men were spread all over town with several roaming the Maryland side. Stevens had gathered about a dozen slaves and armed them with pikes, but the blacks were reluctant to risk the penalty of insurrection—death by hanging. The hostages wandered about inside the Armory gate and wondered why they were there. To their questions, Brown answered, "I came here from Kansas, and this is a slave State; I want to free all the negroes in this State; I have possession now of the United States armory, and if the citizens interfere with me I must only burn the town and have blood."[17]

At dawn townsfolk grabbed old flintlocks and squirrel guns and began firing into the armory. Dr. John Starry rode to Charlestown (now Charles Town, West Virginia), about eight miles away, and hurried two companies of militia to the Ferry. Brown released the B & O train, and it sped off to Baltimore, stopping on the way just long enough for the conductor to wire word of the raid to John W. Garrett, the railroad's president.

At 10:30 a.m. Garrett wired Governor Henry A. Wise of Virginia, Major General George A. Stewart, Maryland Volunteers, and President James Buchanan in Washington: "Insurrection at Harpers Ferry! Send troops!" By noon, militia from Baltimore, Richmond, and all the nearby communities had been alerted and were boarding fast trains to the Ferry. There were no Army troops stationed in Washington. Buchanan was forced to send Colonel Robert E. Lee with a company of marines to recapture the federal armory and arrest the raiders.

While the government mobilized its forces, Brown idled the hours away. He waited for his reinforcements, the imaginary two, three, or four hundred blacks who would rush to his aid, and join together to fight their way into the mountains of Virginia and establish outposts of freedom.

At noon, October 17, militia besieged the armory, driving Brown, nine raiders, and all the hostages and armed slaves into a small brick enginehouse for safety. Escape was no longer possible. The raid had turned deadly. Three townsmen lay dead near the armory yard. Dangerfield Newby, Brown's sole casualty, died instantly when an eight inch spike, fired from a musket, entered his neck. Newby, a free mulatto, lay in an alley, his body mutilated by citizens and feasted upon by hungry hogs that roamed the streets. Before nightfall, Harpers Ferry's well-meaning mayor, Fontaine Beckham, lay dead beside the body of Hayward Shepherd.

Several enterprising railroaders from Martinsburg launched an uncoordinated attack on the enginehouse. Several died in the assault and uncounted others fell from wounds. As the afternoon progressed, Brown's casualties mounted. Two of his sons sustained mortal wounds. Watson, shot under a flag of truce, and Oliver both lay dying by their father's side. Aaron Stevens, shot while escorting a hostage under the white flag, lay bleeding on the floor of the Wager House. Kagi and the men at Hall's Rifle Works lost their lives along the banks of the Shenandoah. By the next morning, Brown had only four men standing at his side in the enginehouse. Hundreds of armed men, many of them drunk, surrounded the remaining survivors and pelleted the enginehouse with musket fire. Late that night Colonel Lee arrived with a company of marines. He closed the bars, and for a few hours all was quiet.

On October 18, shortly after daylight, Colonel Lee sent the marines against the heavy doors of the enginehouse. In less than three minutes they battered through the planks, struck Brown on the head and bayoneted his kidney. The Bluejackets mortally wounded Dauphin Thompson and Jerry Anderson, and captured Edwin Coppoc and Shields Green. A doctor examined both Brown and Aaron Stevens and predicted that they would die of their wounds.[18]

The marines laid the dead and dying, including one of their own, in a lot outside the armory. With bayonets fixed, they formed a hollow square to keep away angry citizens who were intent upon killing the wounded and mutilating the dead. Much to the surprise of those nearby, Brown opened his eyes, looked around, and smiled

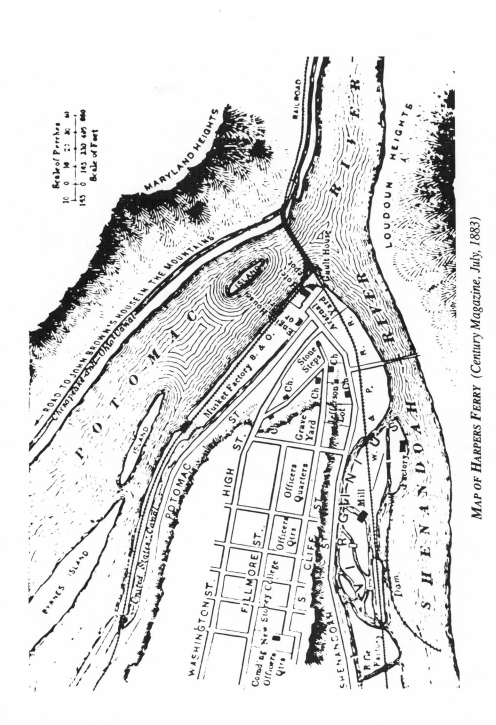

MAP OF HARPERS FERRY (Century Magazine, July, 1883)

HARPERS FERRY: THE FIGHTING AT THE ENGINE HOUSE
(Frank Leslie's Illustrated Newspaper, October, 1859)

STORMING THE ENGINE HOUSE
(Frank Leslie's Illustrated Newspaper, October, 1859)

faintly. Marines formed a heavy guard and rushed Brown and Stevens to the paymaster's office and laid them on cots.

About 1:00 p.m. a train rolled into Harpers Ferry. Governor Henry A. Wise stepped off with Senator James M. Mason and Congressman Charles J. Faulkner, both of Virginia, and Congressman Clement L. Vallandigham of Ohio. When Wise learned Brown was conscious but not expected to live, he led his entourage, which now included reporters, military men, former hostages and local citizens, over to the paymaster's office to hear what might be the raider's last words. Both Wise and Mason were certain that Brown would lead them to influential Northern co-conspirators like Seward, Giddings, Sumner and other Black Republican abolitionists.[19]

Mason led the questioning, and for three hours Brown, battered and bleeding, replied with firm, stinging rebukes, condemning his interrogators for their adherence to slavery.[20]

"Can you tell us, at least," Mason asked, "who furnished the money for your expedition?"

"I furnished most of it myself," Brown replied. "I cannot implicate others. It is by my own folly that I have been taken. I could easily have saved myself from it had I exercised my own better judgment..."

A little later Congressman Vallandigham asked, "Mr. Brown, who sent you here?"

"No man sent me here; it was my own prompting and that of my Maker, or that of the devil, whichever you please to ascribe it to. I acknowledge no man in human form."

THE PRISON, GUARD-HOUSE, AND COURT-HOUSE, CHARLESTOWN, WEST VIRGINIA (*Frank Leslie's Illustrated Newspaper, October, 1859*)

The conversation drifted to the stealing of property and the killing of citizens, and Mason wanted to know: "How do you justify your acts?"

"I think," Brown replied, "you are guilty of a great wrong against God and humanity—I say it without wishing to be offensive—and it would be perfectly right in any one to interfere with you so far as to free those you willfully and wickedly hold in bondage. I do not say this insultingly."

Wise had invited several reporters to hear the questioning because he wanted Brown's confession given the widest possible publicity. Throughout the session, they squeezed closer to the center of the room, scribbling notes as fast as they could take them. Brown addressed most of his answers to the press, knowing that everything he said would make headline news in the North. But he was a little startled when a bystander said, "The New York *Herald* of yesterday, in speaking of this affair, mentions a letter in this way: 'Apropos of this exciting news, we recollect a very significant passage in one of Gerrit Smith's letters, published a month or two ago, in which he speaks of the folly of attempting to strike the shackles off the slaves by the force of moral suasion or legal agitation, and predicts that the next movement made in the direction of negro emancipation would be an insurrection in the South.'"[21]

Brown said he had not seen the *Herald* for several days, but he agreed with "Mr. Smith that moral suasion is hopeless. I don't think the people of the slave States will ever consider the subject of slavery in its true light till some other argument is resorted to than moral suasion." On October 18, even as Brown spoke, an editorial in the *Herald* asked, "Is this the first act in the programme?—and are those white abolitionists spoken of in our despatches emissaries of the peaceful Gerrit?"

But Mason and Vallandigham were not interested in Gerrit Smith, or for that matter, anyone else connected with the Secret Six. They knew where Smith stood and had listened for years to what they considered to be his constantly shifting blusterings. To them, Smith was merely a nuisance and an abolitionist whose modest political power stemmed from his great wealth. Gerrit Smith had not aligned himself with the Republican Party, and he posed no threat to the Southern Democrats. His implication in Brown's raid would produce little, if any, political capital. As Mason, Wise and others sifted through the haystack for accomplices, men like Smith were discarded as politically unimportant chaff.[22]

Vallandigham switched the questioning back to the main issue. "Did you expect a general rising of the slaves in case of your success?"

"No, sir; nor did I wish it," Brown lied deliberately. "I expected to gather them up from time to time and set them free."

Another bystander declared, "To set them free would sacrifice the life of every man in this community."

"I do not think so."

"I know it. I think you are fanatical."

"And I think you are fanatical. 'Whom the gods would destroy they first make mad,' and you are mad."

When Brown was asked how he obtained so many guns, he replied, "I bought them," and when someone asked from whom, he refused to tell them.

A reporter then asked him if he had anything further to say, and Brown, now confident that martyrdom was but hours away, addressed the entire gathering.

I have nothing to say, only that I claim to be here in carrying out a measure I believe perfectly justifiable, and not to act the part of an incendiary or ruffian, but to aid those suffering a great wrong. I wish to say, furthermore, that you had better—all you people at the South—prepare yourselves for a settlement of this question, that must come up for settlement sooner than you are prepared for it. The sooner you are prepared the better. You may dispose of me very easily; I am nearly disposed of now; but this question is still to be settled—this negro question I mean—the end of that is not yet...

Had Gerrit Smith and the Secret Six stood in the paymaster's office during the questioning, they might have departed with deeper admiration for the blood-stained old man who uttered not a word of betrayal, but their peace of mind would have been short-lived. When Governor Wise and his colleagues returned to the Wager House, Colonel Lee greeted them with a carpetbag stuffed with John Brown's documents and correspondence a scouting party had found at the Kennedy house. Wise and Mason dumped the contents on a table in the hotel and out poured a flood of letters from Smith, Sanborn, Stearns, Howe, Higginson, and other influential men who had supported Brown with money or encouragement. On October 20, the news hit New England with dramatic effect. The New York *Herald* declared that Gerrit Smith, Frederick Douglass and Joshua Giddings were all implicated and that Smith had supplied "the sinews of war." In the same issue, the *Herald* reprinted Smith's Jerry Rescue letter and Brown's proposed Provisional Constitution side by side. A day later, the paper editorially accused Smith and Douglass of being "accessories before the fact."[23]

While Brown and the remnants of his Provisional army acclimated themselves to the Charlestown, Virginia, jail, a frightened and distraught Gerrit Smith contemplated his own dismal future. Evidence already published made him an accessory to the same charges levied against Brown; murder, treason and "conspiring and advising with slaves and others to rebel." Frederick Douglass had already fled to Canada. Stearns, Howe, and Sanborn were making plans to follow, and Parker was in his deathbed and safe from arrest in Rome. Only Higginson remained at home and defiantly celebrated Brown's attack on slavery. Edwin Morton, Smith's live-in tutor, sought refuge in England rather than face arrest and be compelled to give damaging testimony.[24]

Smith did not know how many documents found in Brown's carpetbag contained his name or referred to him in some damaging way. For all Smith knew, Brown could have kept an itemized list of every cent donated by himself and of every pledge he ever made. For several days, Smith could not eat, sleep, or think, but he remained lucid enough to rummage through his personal papers and burn every scrap of evidence in his possession associated with Brown's plans. At the same time, he sent his son-in-law, Charles D. Miller, to Boston to destroy evidence there. Miller discovered that Stearns, Howe, and Sanborn had already destroyed most of it. Brown, Stearns and the Boston members of the conspiracy sought legal advice and divided their correspondence into two piles: one contained incriminating evidence, which they destroyed, and the other contained helpful evidence should they be brought to trial.

From Boston, Miller hurried to Ohio, where he sorted through John Brown Jr.'s correspondence and discarded anything damaging. Miller told young Brown that Smith, "was in a very distressed state of mind, fearing that the Government would pounce on him and ruin him, and he wished to destroy any vestige of evidence," that could be used against him.[25]

New letters were delivered to Smith almost as fast as he destroyed old ones, and he barely had the courage to read them. From Cleveland, J. M. Sterling wrote that he expected to hear of Smith's indictment for treason and hoped "that this may be the case and that you thus, may have a chance to talk eloquently to the whole nation."[26]

Smith was not in the mood for eloquence, and any reference to jail terrified him. He wished to talk to no one, much less the whole nation. Then Leonard Gibbs of Greenwich, New York, wrote suggesting that Smith organize a movement to rescue Captain Brown.[27] The proposal, at least to Gibbs, made a lot of sense. If Smith was willing to save Jerry McHenry from slavedom, certainly there was an even more compelling reason to protect John Brown from the gallows. People like W. H. Fish did not understand the trembling emotions of the man in the Peterboro mansion when he jubilantly wrote Smith, "What a stir the Harper's Ferry affair is causing. But I suppose that you are rejoicing in the experience...and I suppose the stir raised against you affects you about as much as they do the everlasting hills."[28]

Smith, who always worked hard and never lacked motivation, began falling apart on October 22 when he read scathing incriminations in the *Herald*. Despite his bombastic outpourings and predictions of war, he had not expected the bloodshed at Harpers Ferry, and because he had destroyed so much of his correspondence, no one can be sure what he did expect, but Gerrit Smith was too frightened and burdened with guilt to think clearly. He consulted Dr. John McCall of Utica, who tried to put Smith's mind at ease by asking Judge Savage if his patient was in any danger of arrest. The judge, who did not know as much about Brown's raid as Smith, assured McCall that there was no reason for anyone to be alarmed. The doctor comforted Smith with the judge's opinion and offered his best medical advice: "Now my friend your trouble of Brain, in not being able to rest at night was occasioned mainly by the constipated state of your bowels"—a condition chronic with the troubled landowner.[29]

In late October, the New York *Herald* sent a special correspondent to Peterboro to get a statement from Smith. As the reporter rode through the village, people told him that Smith was in imminent danger of being kidnapped and carried off to Virginia. In 1858, when Smith had run and lost the race for governor of New York, the same reporter had covered the campaign and was shocked by the sudden change in the usually affable landowner's appearance. Smith had withstood the strain of constant traveling and the customary political mud-slinging with impervious indifference. Now the reporter quickly observed that Smith's reaction to Brown's raid had,

> not only impaired his health; but is likely to seriously affect his excitable and illy-balanced mind. He is a very different man from what he was twelve months since. His calm, dignified, impressive bearing has given way to a hasty, nervous agitation, as though some great fear was constantly before his imagination. His eye is bloodshot and restless as that of a startled horse. He has lost flesh, and his face looks as red and as rough as though he had just returned from one of old Brown's Kansas raids.[30]

Smith refused to discuss Brown, but at times lamented dolefully, "I am going to be indicted, sir, indicted! You must not talk to me about it....If any man in the Union is taken, it will be me."

Since the raid, two attorneys had been constant visitors at the Smith mansion. Charles B. Sedgwick of Syracuse and Timothy Jenkins of Oneida had evidently counseled their client not to talk. They also suggested other precautions, and Smith posted guards around his home. Male occupants on his Peterboro property carried arms by day and slept with their weapons at night. Parcels brought to the house were carefully opened and inspected for explosive devices.[31]

The reporter from the *Herald* made astute observations and summed up his brief interview with Smith by writing:

> He is in evident alarm and agitation, inconsistent with the idea that his complicity with the plot is simply to the extent already made public. I believe that Brown's visit to his house last spring was intimately connected with the insurrection, and that it is the knowledge that at any moment, either by the discovery of papers or the confession of accomplices, his connection with the affair may become exposed, that keeps Mr. Smith in constant excitement and fear.[32]

On November 2, 1859, after a short whirlwind trial, John Brown was sentenced to hang. Through much of the testimony he conducted his own defense from a cot on the floor placed near the center of the courtroom. Five hundred people squeezed into the chamber, most of them standing in hushed silence as Prosecutor Andrew Hunter paraded a host of witnesses by the jury. The verdict was a foregone conclusion. But Brown aimed his defense not at the jury but at the spectators and the press. Each day in court his Old Testament attack on slavery attracted more sympathizers, and those in the gallery who had shouted "Lynch him! Lynch him!" on the first day of the trial listened to the final verdict in hushed whispers. When the old man in the silver whiskers left the courtroom, they stared in silent respect as he hobbled with calm righteousness across the street to his jail cell.

Governor Wise and Senator Mason had followed the trial with growing apprehension. When Brown delivered his final statement to the court, they knew they had created a martyr whose death would bring no end of trouble. Brown had said calmly that he was now "fully persuaded that I am worth inconceivably more to hang than for any other purpose."[33] Even Wise, referring to Brown, admitted, "He is the gamest man I ever saw."[34]

What everyone observed and admired in John Brown was his resolute courage. He believed in his own convictions and had the fortitude to accept the consequences, even if they ended his life. On December 2, as he left his cell for the last time, he stared into the sunlit landscape of western Virginia and seemed shocked by the huge lines of uniformed militia sent by the governor to escort him to the gallows. He turned to his jailer and said calmly, "I had no idea that Governor Wise considered my execution so important."[35] Then he extracted a scrap of paper on which he had scribbled a few immortal words and handed it to the deputy:

> I John Brown am now quite certain that the crimes of this guilty land;
> will never be purged away; but with Blood. I had as I now think; vainly
> flattered myself that without very much bloodshed; it might be done.[36]

Wendell Phillips, the matchless abolitionist orator who knew intimately John Brown, Gerrit Smith, and all the members of the Secret Six, referred to Brown as "that old Puritan Soul," and said that his wonderfully prophetic and imperishable message "melted" a "million hearts" of his countrymen. One heart not melted belonged to Gerrit Smith, who on November 7, 1859, entered the New York State Asylum for the Insane at Utica. The *Herald*, which had maintained an uncanny interest in Smith's convoluted behavior, reported that his case was "one of decided lunacy" and his mind was "considerably disordered." He appeared to be "quite deranged, intellectually as well as morally; and he is also feeble physically."[37]

Underlying Smith's emotional and mental collapse dwelt a deep sense of guilt. Ever since Brown's raid, he had been "haunted with the idea that he was culpably responsible for all the lives that have been and will be sacrificed." For two weeks his personal moral convictions fought an indecisive battle against his faltering courage. He felt compelled to go to Charlestown, surrender to Virginia authorities, and relieve his shattered conscience. Being a deeply religious man, he believed that he deserved punishment for all the lost lives. As a man of deep loyalty, he felt a personal responsibility for Brown's fate, but he shrank from the prospect of personal punishment.

Bouts of delirium gave him escape from this tangle of inner conflicts. His wife and family finally decided he needed rest. They made arrangements to shelter him from anticipated warrants and took him to the State Asylum. When Smith departed for Utica he did so believing he was on his way to Virginia. He remained at the asylum until the end of December. By then John Brown was dead, a great hero to some, a great villain to others, but a martyr to the cause of freedom for the black man.[38]

From birth to death, John Brown's life had been shadowed by failure and disappointment. He had an uncanny ability to bring suffering to everyone who ever associated with him. No one suffered more than his own family, and yet no one believed in him more. His simple Puritanical honesty influenced most people he met who believed deeply in God, and few people were more susceptible to John Brown's compelling incantations than Gerrit Smith. Without Smith's support and that of the members of the Secret Six, Brown might have ended his life as it started— on a farm with a small tanyard.

Had Brown not surveyed a tract of land endowed by Smith to Oberlin College, the bankrupt Ohio land speculator may never have heard of the Peterboro landowner and his generous patrimony to black refugees. Had the great Peterboro moralist and reformer not met John Brown, he would have lived his life with a clear conscience and unabated generosity. But Gerrit Smith had money and, despite the Jerry McHenry rescue, not much courage. Had he openly admitted his relationship to John Brown, he would have shared a part of the glory. Instead he chose ignominy.

When Governor Wise decided to try John Brown in Virginia, he took the matter of treason out of the hands of the federal government. Aside from some embarrassment, Gerrit Smith could not be tried in Virginia unless forcibly kidnapped and taken to Charlestown. Smith had already taken precautions against that possibility.

After Smith came out of the asylum, he lived for fifteen years confronted by the stain of his denial. As time passed, he often referred to John Brown as a great man, but on October 22, 1859, Smith lied about his implication in the "great man's" raid. Now he could not tell the truth, not even to those who knew.

6

Aftermath

On the scaffold, John Brown's death came quickly, or so it seemed. James Redpath, who had walked the prairies of Kansas and Nebraska with the old raider, wrote of his execution:

> There was but one spasmodic effort of the hands to clutch at the neck, but for nearly five minutes the limbs jerked and quivered. He seemed to retain an extraordinary hold on life....After the body had dangled in mid-air for twenty minutes, it was examined by the surgeons for signs of life. First the Charlestown physicians went up and made their examination, and after them the military surgeons....

A small group of doctors could not agree among themselves whether John Brown was dead. After thirty-eight minutes, they cut him down and his body fell in a heap on the scaffold. Once more they listened for a heartbeat and finally pronounced him dead. The body was taken back to the jail for the doctors to sign a death certificate, but when they removed the hood, they were disturbed by his appearance. Unlike a hanged man, his face had not blackened, the eyes did not protrude, and there were no discharges from his nose or mouth. The doctors argued. No one would sign the death certificate. One said he would issue a certificate only if Brown was decapitated. Another suggested they administer a massive dose of strychnine. They decided to go to lunch and give the body time to stiffen. Three and a half hours after the hanging they finally signed the death certificate. The doctors still could not believe that John Brown was dead. Except for his body, they were right.[1]

Brown's body was delivered to his widow at Harpers Ferry and carried from there to his home in North Elba. At each stop along the way, great crowds gathered at train stations to pay homage. Platoons of police pushed back zealous sympathizers, and when the coffin was carried to the Walnut Street wharf in Philadelphia, an honor guard stood watch throughout the night. From New York City to Westport, Kansas, bells tolled as the small procession rolled slowly north. At every stop citizens converged upon the widow's car and expressed words of sympathy. On December 8, 1859, the mortal remains of John Brown were laid to rest in a grave by a great boulder near his still unfinished home. The huge stone still stands, not far from towering White Face Mountain, and represents, as Oswald Garrison Villard wrote, "the best possible monument to the native ruggedness and steadfastness of his character."[2]

A small gathering of family and friends attended the burial, including Reverend Joshua Young of Burlington, Vermont, J. Miller McKim, of Philadelphia, and Wendell Phillips, who had followed Brown's career with outspoken admiration. Noticeably absent were members of the Secret Six, especially Gerrit Smith, on whose land John Brown had chosen to live and someday "rest his bones.

At noon that day, thousands of people left their places of work to sit for hours in church, listen to commemorative services, and bear witness to Brown's "sublime purpose." In the Western Reserve, where people remembered John Brown as a kind, honest, and inept businessman, stores and public offices closed for the day, and in Cleveland banners stretched across the streets proclaiming: "I cannot better serve the cause I love than die for it." Reverend J. C. White reminded his congregation what John Brown had so many times said: "Without the shedding of blood, there can be no remission of such a sin." An uncompromising resolution was adopted and signed: "The irrepressible conflict is upon us, and it will never end until Freedom or slavery go to the wall. In such a contest and under such dire necessity we say 'without fear and without reproach' let freedom stand and the Union be dissolved." Already, even before his lifeless body was laid to rest, John Brown's soul was marching on. Frail and fearful, Gerrit Smith deprived himself of a distinguished place in the history he helped to create.[3]

Dr. John P. Gray, in charge of the asylum at Utica, referred to the Harpers Ferry affair as "the last straw" in a progression of events that resulted in Smith's breakdown. He blamed the unsuccessful gubernatorial campaign of 1858 as the genesis of Smith's problem, followed by attacks of "serious indigestion and sympathetic disturbances of the heart." He believed Smith suffered from dyspepsia, periods of deep depression, and "intellectual exaltation only to be accounted for on the theory of then existing cerebral disturbance and the approach of serious brain trouble." Unlike McCall's earlier diagnosis, constipation was not mentioned as disturbing the brain. After giving so serious a diagnosis, neither Dr. Gray nor close friends could explain Gerrit Smith's rapid recovery. His wife joined him for Thanksgiving dinner at the asylum and four weeks later he was back in Peterboro practicing his profession.[4]

The illness spared Smith from testifying before the Mason Committee. Because Governor Wise tried Brown in Virginia, Senator Mason had not been able to identify the Black Republicans whom he was certain had financed the raid. On December 14, the United States Senate selected a committee to determine "whether any citizens of the United States not present were implicated therein, or accessory thereto, by contributions of money, arms, munitions, or otherwise." With Mason as chairman, the committee initiated its investigations on January 4, 1860, and summoned, among others, Sanborn, Stearns, Morton, Howe, and Gerrit Smith. Sanborn refused to testify, and when deputies came to Concord to arrest him, he clung to a post on his porch until neighbors arrived with weapons and escorted the lawmen out of town. Finally, on March 21, Smith agreed to testify providing the committee would first confer with Dr. Gray. Gray, of course, declared that Smith's health would be jeopardized if he was forced to go to Washington. By then both Stearns and Howe had testified, and Mason had not been able to implicate his Republican enemies. He graciously excused Smith because "his health was such as to render it improper to bring him here."[5]

Two weeks after the Mason Committee excused Smith, he wrote Senator Charles Sumner, "Now, through great mercy, I am in good health." Five days after Mason concluded his investigation, Congressman John Cochrane, Smith's nephew, expressed delight at his uncle's "entire restoration to health."[6]

Smith's first denial of complicity came shortly after the news of Brown's raid hit the streets. Three New York Democrats, Watts Sherman, Royal Phelps, and S. L. M. Barlow, calling themselves members of the Vigilant Association, printed a long address entitled the "Rise and Progress of the Harpers Ferry Rebellion." They claimed the raid was the work of a secret society. Gerrit Smith was the central figure and the society, with Smith's endorsement and money, advocated the use of force against slavery and repudiated any law supporting it. Smith denied the charges and demanded a public retraction. When the three accusers refused, Smith hired the firm of Sedgwick, Andrews and Kennedy to sue Sherman, Phelps, and Barlow for fifty thousand dollars each.[7]

Smith, however, could not refute some of the statements made by the trio because he had destroyed most of his correspondence. Nonetheless, on May 22, 1860, the New York *Herald* printed a three-column letter from Smith in which he denied again any complicity in the Harpers Ferry conspiracy. He accused the *Herald* of suggesting that the attack had been "concocted under my roof." He admitted that "John Brown was at my house but once in the year 1859, and then only for a day and a half. He was on his way from Kansas to his home." Smith did not mention two important meetings held there in 1858, nor anything of the money he pumped into Brown's project. He then assailed the Vigilant Association for libelously publishing "the meanest, nakedest, and most atrocious lies." All the denials appeared in the press while the Mason Committee was still hearing testimony and before Smith's libel suits came to trial.[8]

Smith decided that Sedgwick needed help prosecuting his suit against Sherman, Phelps and Barlow. In March, 1860, he hired abolitionist Lysander Spooner. He may not have known that two weeks before John Brown's death, Spooner and Higginson had planned to kidnap Governor Wise and hold him hostage in exchange for Brown's release. Lack of funds, the scourge of John Brown's life, prevented the attempt. Nonetheless, Spooner and Sedgwick could not agree on who to sue: the three men for libel, the entire Vigilant Association, the *Herald,* the *Journal of Commerce*, or everyone.

Spooner warned Smith that he would not win the suit against the newspapers, so in October, 1860, he went to New York and interviewed the three members of the Vigilant Association. He advised Smith that the defense would probably attempt "to prove that you have either counselled, or participated in, movements so nearly like those charged, that little or no essential injustice has been done, and that you ought to recover but small damages, if any."[9]

Spooner's report shocked Smith, and he immediately began a discretionary retreat. The last thing Smith wanted was to have skillful lawyers digging into his past relationship with Brown before a jury and the general public. Spooner may not have wanted his own schemes subject to scrutiny. Smith's illness had saved him from a confrontation with the Mason Committee. Now Barlow stood ready to prove before a court that Smith had "counselled or participated" in the allegations charged. Since Phelps and Sherman had already agreed to print a retraction, Barlow condescendingly followed, and Smith barely escaped the embarrassing hazards of a trial.[10] He also lost another opportunity to clean the slate by admitting his support of Brown and enjoying some of the credit for financing the fight for emancipation.

Strangely enough, Smith's errant suit against Sherman, Phelps, and Barlow did not teach him to ignore slurs and accusations regarding his relationship with Brown. Five years later (June, 1865) at a time when he was lobbying for the release of ex-Confederate President Jefferson Davis, the Chicago *Tribune* published an insulting article. "Gerrit Smith stands indebted to his sire for a feeble intellect and a large fortune." Born a coward, he "has none of the stuff of which men are made." The *Tribune*, which now had more information on Smith's complicity in the raid, wrote that after Brown's arrest, Smith "became insane, took refuge in a lunatic asylum and remained there until Lincoln was inaugurated."[11]

In November, 1865, when Smith discovered the existence of the article, he went to Chicago, demanded a retraction, and threatened a libel suit if a public apology was not printed. He stipulated that the *Tribune's* published apology must repudiate all the "numerous gross, and cruel falsehoods" reported, and be satisfactory to himself. The paper must make it clear to its readers that Smith did not feign insanity but had become badly disoriented, did not know one person from the other, and had been on the threshold of death. He also wanted his length of stay in the asylum corrected to one month, compared with seventeen months alleged by the *Tribune*.

Horace White, editor of the *Tribune*, ignored Smith's demands. He further aggravated the landowner by declaring that the article had not accused Smith of feigning insanity but reported that he had become insane. White apparently had little fear of Smith's threats. He not only refused to print a retraction, he reprinted the entire article, adding that for Smith to sue the *Tribune* on the basis of that one article proved that Smith was not only "then insane, but that he had never been cured." Smith had no recourse but to sue or look foolish, and in December, 1865, William W. Farwell brought suit against the *Tribune* for $50,000.00. White once again republished the complete article, this time adding his own comments: "We have never seen Mr. Smith in an insane asylum, but we expect to, before he [collects] his $50,000.00."[12]

The editor of the Albany *Argus* sided with White and wrote: "If Smith wants to prove that he was insane, and is not quite recovered, let him stick to his suit. He has been a newspaper parasite all his life; and this attempt to get *damages* out of a publisher will only damage himself."[13]

White was smart enough to stall the suit and give himself time to dig for sufficient evidence to fully justify the article. Not until October, 1866, did Judge Drummond, of the Federal District Court of Illinois, hear arguments presented by both attorneys. He ruled that the charge of feigning insanity to escape danger would not furnish grounds for further action unless the article in question also alleged that Smith deserved punishment from which his insanity saved him. Drummond's ruling forced both sides to investigate the whole story of John Brown's raid, and of Smith's possible complicity.[14]

Smith felt threatened and again retained Charles B. Sedgwick to assist Farwell, suggesting that a way be found to settle the suit out of court. On the other side, Horace White pushed to have the case heard. In January, 1867, he filed a formal plea in answer to the charge of libel. The argument of the case now shifted to whether Smith had aided Brown in Kansas and Harpers Ferry, and if upon Brown's arrest, Smith had taken refuge in a lunatic asylum. The *Tribune's* attorneys had compiled numerous reports, articles and documents showing that Smith's interest in and support of Brown's projects went far beyond casual or incidental involvement. The *Tribune* knew it had erred in accusing Smith of feigned insanity. White concentrated on discrediting Smith before a jury by forcing him to deny his patronage of Brown. By now White was certain he had enough information to prove Smith's implication in the Harpers Ferry raid. He also was convinced that Smith did not want his relationship with Brown subjected to minute investigation by a jury. Smith was beginning to manifest signs of returning dementia, but he was also a proud and somewhat confused man. He was not yet willing to drop his suit but he was willing to settle for less. He asked Sedgwick to talk to the *Tribune*. In exchange for an adequate and ample retraction, he would drop the suit.[15]

Sedgwick went to Utica to obtain evidence from Dr. Gray and others attesting to Smith's insanity. Smith reviewed Sedgwick's findings before the attorney departed for Chicago. He was so shocked by the facts that he slumped into depression. Dr. Gray feared another breakdown and told Smith's grandson to remove razors and weapons from the house because his grandfather might commit suicide. The case was scheduled for trial in October, 1867, but Smith gathered himself together and in July went to Chicago in an effort to personally settle out of court. Horace White was out of the office, and Smith convinced the editor in charge to print a satisfactory recantation. On July 27, 1867, the *Tribune* announced the settlement of the Gerrit Smith libel suit. It again reprinted the entire article, expressed regret for its implied charge that Smith feigned insanity, and admitted that competent medical testimony proved that he had been actually insane.[16]

When White returned to the office one week later, he published a statement declaring that the suit had been settled during his absence and in violation of his wishes. Disregarding the matter of Smith's insanity, he wrote:

> Now I am in possession of information which enables me to affirm that Mr. Gerrit Smith was fully advised of John Brown's purpose to make an armed invasion or raid upon Virginia, for a long time prior to such invasion or raid; that...Smith assented to and co-operated in such invasion or raid, with advice, money, and counsel; that interviews took place between John Brown and Gerrit Smith at the residence of the latter in Peterboro...in the summer of 1859,

at which time Brown fully disclosed his plans.[17] With the exception of the date, White's statement was correct. He had obtained the information from John Brown Jr. at his home in Sandusky, Ohio.[18]

JOHN BROWN'S HOME, NORTH ELBA, NY
(Library of Congress)

Once again Smith lapsed into mental and emotional anguish. He later wrote an account of his relations with Brown which directly contradicted unimpeachable documentary evidence.[19] Again Smith asked White for a retraction. White did not comply, but he did have the last word: "As I have not charged you with falsehood, I do not see why I should retract such a charge. I stated certain facts which I am able to prove." In closing, he added rather proudly, "I was a friend of John Brown during his life-time, and I honor his memory as much as any man."[20] Undoubtedly, Smith felt the sting of Horace White's proud confession.

In retrospect, there is no doubt that Smith became emotionally tormented by the news of John Brown's raid, but the cause, or causes, are not so clear. Prior to running for governor in 1858, he suffered from a serious attack of typhoid fever, but he seemed to have recovered his health in time to conduct a rigorous but losing campaign. Judging from his enormous accumulation of correspondence, all in his own hand, he seemed vigorously at work and in a normal state of health throughout September, 1859. Hiram Corliss had visited him on the 29th of that month and a few days later wrote a note thanking the Smiths for their gracious hospitality. Gerrit's friends knew of his preoccupation with health because he openly discussed it, and no one would have failed to wish him well if they suspected he was ill. Until October 17, 1858, the day John Brown's raid first hit the news stands, Smith continued to endorse his correspondence in a normal manner. He endorsed one letter on the 18th and another on the 21st. His next endorsement did not appear until December 5, three days after John Brown's death. There is no indication that Smith suffered any mental or emotional strain prior to October 17. If he did, the association of his name with John Brown's raid decidedly contributed to his sudden mental instability. For the balance of his life he seemed quite normal, except when the specter of John Brown threatened again to disrupt his public image and expose the truth.[21]

JOHN BROWN'S GRAVE STONE, NORTH ELBA, NY
(U.S. Army Military History Institute)

Whether touched by unremitted guilt or the approach of old age, Smith turned once more to religion. Still, he could not bring himself to the point of admitting he had helped John Brown. The Civil War had ended, emancipation had freed the slaves, and nobody but Gerrit Smith really cared any more whether the wealthy landowner from Peterboro had supported Brown.

In 1872 Franklin Sanborn began collecting letters and documents for his *Life and Letters of John Brown*. He asked Smith if he did not think it was time to publish whatever was known of John Brown's plans, as those who once knew the raider were passing away. Mrs. Smith replied, deprecating any unnecessary use of names, warning that excessive disclosures could revive her husband's "mental excitement." On October 19, 1872, Smith confirmed that he was "not competent to advise in the case." He added, "From that day to this, I have had but a hazy view of dear John Brown's great work." Perhaps if Smith had not destroyed at least twelve letters from John Brown written between June, 1857, and June, 1859, his memory would have been less hazy.

GERRIT SMITH—LATTER YEARS
(Madison County Historical Society, Oneida, NY)

Normally, Smith saved all his correspondence. His files for 1858 and 1859 contained over eight hundred letters, but those from Brown were all purged and destroyed in the fall of 1859. Smith closed his note to Sanborn with a plea that the "full history of the transaction" not be published until after his death, or if a book was published prior to his death, that his name be used as sparingly as possible. To Sanborn, at least, Smith was finally able to admit that "dear John Brown" had done "great work."[22]

When Gerrit Smith died suddenly on December 28, 1874, he was remembered for his great patrimony. The New York *Evening Mail* ran a leading editorial describing him as

> one of the greatest and best men who has been reared on American soil and has illustrated the value of American institutions. It has been a long, noble, and useful career—without a blemish on any part of it; one of sustained and natural dignity, one that did not need the adventitious aid of high

political stations. A mind more hospitable to new ideas, more thoroughly imbued with Democratic principles, more vigorous in the unselfish service of the race—has not been known in this country.[23]

The New York *Times* printed a three-column notice placing Smith "in the front rank of the men whose influence was most felt" in building the national life of America." The New York *Independent* devoted the whole front page to a summary of his career. The account was written by Senator Henry Wilson of Massachusetts who knew of John Brown's intimate relationship with Smith and the Secret Six. Yet no national newspaper, not even the *Emancipator*, the *Liberator* or the *National Era*, which heaped praise upon Smith, ever mentioned his relationship to Brown, although by then it was common knowledge. At the age of seventy-seven, Gerrit Smith died with his guilt and those who eulogized him respected his wishes. Courage may have failed him in October, 1859, and for the years that followed, but this one frail disruption would not be allowed to eradicate his marvelous record of reform and his sincere desire for full emancipation.[24]

In deference to Smith's wishes, and out of respect for the man himself, Franklin Sanborn kept his pledge of silence until after Smith's death. When Octavius Brooks Frothingham published Gerrit Smith's first biography in 1878 and whitewashed his relationship with John Brown, Sanborn could desist no longer. After publishing the *Life and Letters of John Brown* in 1885, the first clear account of Smith's relationship with Brown, Sanborn discovered that some of the public doubted Smith's involvement. Thirty years after Smith's death, Sanborn was still writing about the meeting in the Peterboro mansion in February, 1858, and again with the Secret Six in Boston's Revere House:

> I do not mean that every detail of those plans was then, or afterwards, talked over between Mr. Smith and myself; but I do mean that we talked, or heard John Brown talk, on the subject...for probably more than ten hours; until the general features of his enterprise became as well known to me, and, as I always supposed, to Mr. Smith, as are the general scope and methods of most undertakings in which men deliberately engage.[25]

Gerrit Smith gave his money to the cause of freedom, denied it, and was called by most of those who knew him a great man. John Brown gave his life to the cause of black freedom and was called a great martyr. If the courts of Virginia were right in pronouncing Brown guilty of conspiracy, murder, and treason, Gerrit Smith was equally culpable and an accessory before the fact. Brown died alone because he wanted to. For fifteen years, Gerrit Smith lived in silence and painfully sheltered his guilt. For greatness, each man paid a penalty, one with his life and the other with a measure of his self-respect.

Appendix

SAMBO'S MISTAKES

In 1848 or 1849, John Brown, posing as a Negro author named Sambo, contributed this document to *The Ram's Head*, a little-known Abolition newspaper published and edited by a small group of free blacks in New York. At the time, Brown was mingling with the small black community in Springfield, Massachusetts. The short essay not only reveals Brown's observations of black behavior but discloses some of his own prejudices regarding politics, religious denominations and civic organizations.

The original document is preserved in the Maryland Historical Society.

Chap 1st

Sambo's Mistakes   For the *Rams Horn*

Mess Editors: Notwithstanding I may have committed a few mistakes in the course of a long life like others of my colored brethren yet you will perceive at a glance that I have always been remarkable for a seasonable discovery of my errors and quick perception of the true course. I propose to give you a few illustrations in this and the following chapters. For instance when I was a boy I learned to read but instead of giving my attention to sacred and profane history by which I might have become acquainted with the true character of God & of man [and] learned the true course for individuals, societies & nations to pursue [and] stored my mind with an endless variety of rational and practical ideas, profited by the experience of millions of others of all ages, fitted myself for the most important stations in life, & fortified my mind with the best and wisest resolutions, & noblest sentiments, & motives, [instead] I have spent my whole life devouring silly novels & other miserable trash such as most of the newspapers of the day & other popular writings are filled with, thereby unfitting myself for the realities of life & acquiring a taste for nonsense & low wit, so that I have no rellish for sober truth, useful knowledge or practical wisdom. By this means I have passed through life without profit to myself or others, a mere blank upon which nothing worth peruseing is written. But I can see in a twink where I missed it. Another error into which I fell in early life was the notion that chewing & smoking tobacco would make a man of me but little inferior to some of the whites. The money I spent in this way would with the interest of it have enabled me to have relieved a great many sufferers supplyed me with a well selected interesting library, & pa[i]d for a good farm for the support & comfort of my old age; whereas I have now neith[er] books, clothing, the satisfaction of having benefited others nor wher[e] to lay my hoary head. Another of the few errors of my life is that I have joined the Free Masons Odd Fellows Sons of Temperance, & a score of other secret societies instead of seeking the company of intelligent wise & good men from whom I might have learned much that would be interesting, instructive, & useful & have in that way squandered a great amount of most precious time, & money enough sometimes in a single year which if I had then put the same out on interest and kept it so would have kept me always above board [and] given me character, & influence amongst men, or have enabled me to pursue some respectable calling, so that I might employ others to their benefit & improvement, but as it is I have always been poor, in debt, & now obliged to travel about in search of employment as a hostler shoeblack & fiddler. But I retain all my quickness of perception [because] I can see readily where I missed it.

Chap 2nd

Sambo's Mistakes

Another error of my riper years has been that when any meeting of colored people has been called in order to consider of any important matter of general interest I have been so eager to display my sprouting talents & so tenacious of some trifling theory or other that I have adopted that I have generally lost all sight of the business in hand [and] consumed the time disputing about things of no moment & thereby defeated entirely many important measures calculated to promote the general welfare; but I am happy to say I can see in a minute where I missed it. Another little fault which I have committed is that if in anything another man has failed of coming up to my standard, notwithstanding he might possess many of the most valuable traits & be most admirably adapted to fill some one important post, I would reject him entirely, injure his influence, oppose his measures, and even glory in his defeats while his intentions were good, & his plans well laid. But I have the great satisfaction of being able to say without fear of intradiction that I can see *verry quick* where *I* missed it.

To be continued.

Chap 3rd

Sambo's Mistakes

Another small mistake which I have made is that I could never bring myself to practise any present self denial although my theories have been excellent. For instance I have bought expensive gay clothing, nice Canes, Watches, safety Chains, Finger-rings, Breast Pins & many other things of a like nature, thinking I might by that means distinguish myself from the vulgar, as some of the better class of whites do. I have always been of the foremost in getting up expensive parties, & running after expensive amusements, and have indulged my appetite freely whenever I had the means (& even with borro[w]ed means) have patronized the dealers in Nuts, Candy, etc., freely & have sometimes bought good suppers & was always a regular customer at Livery stables. By these & many other means I have been unable to benefit my suffering Brethren, & am now but poorly able to keep my own Soul and boddy together; but do not think me thoughtless or dull of apprehention, for I can see at once where I missed it.

Another trifling error of my life has been that I have always expected to secure the favor of the whites by tamely submitting to every species of indignity contempt & wrong, insted of nobly resisting their brutal aggression from principle & taking my place as a man & assuming the responsibilities of a man, a citizen, a husband, a father, a brother, a neighbor, a friend as God required of every one (if his neighbor will allow him to do it;) but I find that I get for all my submission about the same reward that the Southern Slaveocrats render to the Dough-faced Statesmen of the North for being bribed & browbeat, & fooled & cheated, as the Whigs & Democrats love to be, & think themselves highly honored if they may be allowed to lick up the spittle of a Southerner. I say I get the same reward. But I am uncomm[on] quick sighted I can see in a minute where I missed it. Another little blunder I made is, that while I have always been a most zealous Abolitionist I have been constantly at war with my friends about certain religious tenets. I was first a Presbyterian, but I could never think of acting with my Quaker friends for they were the rankest heretiks & the Baptists would be in the water, & the Methodists denied the doctrine of Election, etc. & later years since becoming enlightened by Garrison, Abby Kelly and other really benevolent persons I have been spending all my force on my friends who love the Sabbath, & have felt that all was at stake on that point just as it has proved to be of late in France in the abolition of Slavery in their colonies. Now I cannot doubt, Mess Editors, notwithstanding I have been unsuccessful, that you will allow me full credit for my *peculiar* quick-sightedness. I can see in one second where I missed it.

Author's note: The misspelled words are part of the original essay, and except for omitted letters in a word, I have left them as they were spelled by John Brown.)

WORDS OF ADVICE

At the time John Brown wrote "Words of Advice," he was living alone in Springfield, Massachusetts, and involved in the unpleasant activity of settling suits against Perkins & Brown's defunct wool business. After the passage of the Fugitive Slave Act in 1850, Brown tried to organize the forty odd black families living in Springfield to defend themselves against slave-catchers. He had hoped to expand the organization from Springfield to other cities across the North, but he had accounts to settle and suits to defend. Like many other projects initiated by John Brown, this, too, lasted little longer than the time taken for its creation.

After writing "Sambo's Mistakes" two years earlier, Brown attempted to unify black families to forcibly resist white oppression. After denouncing negroes for cultural supineness and submitting to the sins of temptation, he now takes the Fugitive Slave Act and uses it to bolster the backbone of the black community by organizing them into units of mutual support. In essence, the Act became his catalyst for inducing cultural change and his League of Gileadites became the method. In 1848, John Brown might have been satisfied to settle on the farm he purchased from Gerrit Smith and become a shepherd to the poor black families living in "Timbucto." But in 1851, neither of those men could accept a law that returned men to slavery.

WORDS OF ADVICE

Branch of the United States League of Gileadites. Adopted Jan. 15, 1851, as written and recommended by John Brown.

"UNION IS STRENGTH"

Nothing so charms the American people as personal bravery. Witness the case of Cinques, of everlasting memory, on board the "Amistad." The trial for life of one bold and to some extent successful man, for defending his rights in good earnest, would arouse more sympathy throughout the nation than the accumulated wrongs and sufferings of more than three million of our submissive colored population. We need not mention the Greeks struggling against the oppressive Turks, the Poles against Russia, nor the Hungarians against Austria and Russia combined, to prove this. *No jury can be found in the Northern States that would convict a man for defending his rights to the last extremity. This is well understood by Southern Congressmen, who insisted that the right of trial by jury should not be granted to the fugitive.* Colored people have ten times the number of fast friends among the whites than they suppose, and would have ten times the number they now have were they but half as much in earnest to secure their dearest rights as they are to ape the follies and extravagances of their white neighbors, and to indulge in idle show, in ease, and in luxury. Just think of the money expended by individuals in your behalf in the past twenty years! Think of the number who have been mobbed and imprisoned on your account! Have any of you seen the Branded Hand? Do you remember the names of Lovejoy and Torrey?

Should one of your number be arrested, you must collect together as quickly as possible, so as to outnumber your adversaries who are taking an active part against you. Let no able-bodied man appear on the ground unequipped, or with his weapons exposed to view: let that be understood beforehand. Your plans must be known only to yourself, and with the understanding that all traitors must die, wherever caught and proven guilty. "Whosoever is fearful or afraid, let him return and part early from Mount Gilead" (Judges, vii. 3; Deut. xx. 8). Give all cowards an opportunity to show it on condition of holding their peace. *Do not delay one moment after you are ready: you will lose all your resolution if you do. Let the first blow be the signal for all to engage; and when engaged do not do your work by halves, but make clean work with your enemies,—and be sure you meddle not with any others.* By going about your business quietly, you will get the job disposed of before the number that an uproar would bring together can collect; and you will have the advantage of those who come out against you, for they will be wholly unprepared with either equipments or matured plans; all with them will be confusion and terror. Your enemies will be slow to attack you after you have done up the work nicely; and if they should, they will have to encounter your white friends as well as you; for you may safely calculate on a division of the whites, and may by that means get to an honorable parley.

Be firm, determined, and cool; but let it be understood that you are not to be driven to desperation without making it an awful dear job to others as well as to you. Give them to know distinctly that those who live in wooden houses should not throw fire, and that you are just as able to suffer as your white neighbors. *After effecting a rescue, if you are assailed, go into the houses of your most prominent and influential white friends with your wives; and that will effectually fasten upon them the suspicion of being connected with you, and will compel them to make a common cause with you, whether they would otherwise live up to their profession or not. This would leave them no choice in the matter.* Some would doubtless prove themselves true of their own choice; others would flinch. That would be taking them at their own words. You may make a tumult in the court-room where a trail is going on, by burning gunpowder freely in paper packages, if you cannot think of any better way to create a momentary alarm, and might possibly give one or more of your enemies a hoist. But in such case the prisoner will need to take the hint at once, and bestir himself; and so should his friends improve the opportunity for a general rush.

A lasso might possibly be applied to a slave-catcher for once with good effect. Hold on to your weapons, and never be persuaded to leave them, part with them, or have them far away from you. *Stand by one another and by your friends, while a drop of blood remains; and be hanged, if you must, but tell no tales out of school. Make no confession.*

Union is strength. Without some well-digested arrangements nothing to any good purpose is likely to be done, let the demand be never so great. Witness the case of Hamlet and Long in New York, when there was no well-defined plan of operations or suitable preparation beforehand.

The desired end may be effectually secured by the means proposed; namely, the enjoyment of our inalienable rights.

AGREEMENT

As citizens of the United States of America, trusting in a just and merciful God, whose spirit and all-powerful aid we humbly implore, *we will ever be true to the flag of our beloved country, always acting under it.* We, whose names are hereunto affixed, do constitute ourselves a branch of the United States League of Gileadites. That we will provide ourselves at once with suitable implements, and will aid those who do not possess the means, if any such are disposed to join us. We invite every colored person whose heart is engaged in the performance of our business, whether male or female, old or young. The duty of the aged, infirm, and young members of the League shall be to give instant notice to all members in case of an attack upon any of our people. We agree to have no officers except a treasurer and secretary *pro tem*, until after some trial of courage and talent of able-bodied members shall enable us to elect officers from those who shall have rendered the most important services. Nothing but wisdom and undaunted courage, efficiency, and general good conduct shall in any way influence us in electing our officers.

❖ ❖ ❖

The document ended with nine resolutions giving further emphasis to the "Words of Advice." It was signed by forty-four members. With this support from the black community in Springfield, it was natural for John Brown to believe that if he provided the leadership and the weapons, northern freedmen and southern slaves would join his little army at Harpers Ferry. If he had any doubts, he did not share them with Gerrit Smith and the Secret Six.

The manuscripts for both "Sambo's Mistakes" and "Words of Advice" can be found in Franklin B. Sanborn, *The Life and Letters of John Brown* (Boston: 1891), 124-131.

Notes

ABBREVIATIONS TO NOTES:

AUL   - Atlanta University Library, Atlanta, Georgia
BPL   - Boston Public Library, Boston, MA.
CUL   - Columbia University Library, New York, NY.
HLHU - Houghton Library, Harvard University, Cambridge, MA.
HL   - Huntington Library, Charleston, West Virginia.
ISHL - Illinois State Historical Library, Springfield, IL.
KSHS - Kansas State Historical Society, Topeka, KS.
LC   - Library of Congress, Washington, D. C.
MHS - Massachusetts Historical Society, Boston, MA.
NYPL - New York Public Library, New York, NY.
OHS - Ohio Historical Society, Columbus, OH.
OPL - Omaha Public Library, Omaha, NE.
PHS - Pennsylvania Historical Society, Philadelphia, PA.
SUL   - Syracuse University Library, Syracuse, NY.
UK   - University of Kansas, Lawrence, KS.

Chapter One

1.   Oswald Garrison Villard, *John Brown, 1800-1859: A Biography Fifty Years After* (Boston, 1910), 57-59; Robert Penn Warren, *John Brown: The Making of a Martyr* (New York, 1929), 49-52, 55-56; E. C. Leonard recollections in Franklin B. Sanborn, *The Life and Letters of John Brown* (Boston, 1885), 64-65.
2.   James Redpath, *The Public Life of Captain John Brown* (Boston, 1860), 36.
3.   Richard O. Boyer, *The Legend of John Brown: A Biography and a History* (New York, 1973), 202-205; Sanborn, Life and Letters, 31-32; Villard, John Brown, 17.
4.   Foreman to Redpath, December 28, 1959, Brown Papers, KSHS. For many years, James Foreman worked for the Browns, followed John into Crawford County, Pennsylvania, and helped to build his house and supervise his tannery.
5.   Sanborn, *Life and Letters*, 35; John Jr. was born July 25, 1821, Jason on Jan. 19, 1823, and Owen on Nov. 4, 1824, all in Hudson, Ohio.
6.   Redpath, *Public Life*, 40; In New Richmond, Crawford County, Frederick (1st) was born Jan. 9, 1827, Ruth on Feb. 18, 1829, and Frederick (2nd) on Dec. 31, 1830. Frederick (2nd) had been renamed after the 1st died in March, 1831.

7. Villard, *John Brown*, 24-25, from Miss Sarah Brown's recollections, Villard collection, CUL; See also Boyer, *Legend of John Brown*, 250-252.
8. Sanborn, *Life and Letters*, 43; Warren, *John Brown*, 29.
9. Sanborn, *Life and Letters*, 40-41; John Brown to his brother Frederick, Nov. 21, 1834.
10. *Ibid.*, 42.
11. Brown to Thompson, Oct. 24, 1835, Brown-Thompson Letters, AUL. The Brown-Thompson correspondence has been extensively researched by Richard Boyer. Villard's research is based upon an article in the Kent (Ohio) Courier, September 14, 1906, which agrees on some points and differs on others. Prior to the discovery of the Slaughter Collection, this period of Brown's life relied mainly on Brown's correspondence and Villard's sources; Boyer, *Legend of John Brown*, 265-266.
12. *Ibid.*, 266-267.
13. R. Carlyle Buley, *The Old Northwest: Pioneer Period, 1815-1840*, 2 vols. (Bloomington, IN, 1951), I, 563.
14. Boyer, *Legend of John Brown*, 268.
15. *Ibid.*, 270.
16. Sanborn, *Life and Letters*, 87; Stephen B. Oates, *To Purge This Land With Blood* (Amherst, MA, 1970), 35; Boyer, *Legend of John Brown*, 271.
17. *Ibid.*, 272-73.
18. Villard, *John Brown*, 28, from the Kent *Courier* of Sept. 14, 1906 in the Villard collection.
19. Sanborn, *Life and Letters*, 52-53. John Brown Jr. related the story in a letter, giving the date of 1837. The incident probably occurred in 1836.
20. Brown to Thompson, July 20, 1836; Brown-Thompson Letters, AUL; Boyer, *Legend of John Brown*, 275.
21. *Ibid.*, 276.
22. By the end of 1837, Mary had given birth to four children, Sarah (May 11, 1834), Watson (Oct. 7, 1835), Salmon (Oct. 2, 1836), and Charles (Nov. 3, 1837), bringing the number of children in the family to nine.
23. Villard, *John Brown*, 37-41. John Brown Jr's. account is in the Villard collection, CUL. At times, three sons were involved in the defense of the shanty, John Jr., Jason and Owen, then nineteen, seventeen and sixteen respectively. See also John Brown to John Jr., Jan. 11, 1844, OHS; Boyer, *Legend of John Brown*, 337-339; Warren, *John Brown*, 45-47.
24. Villard, *John Brown*, 29; Boyer, *Legend of John Brown*, 323-324.
25. *Ibid.*, 326-329; Brown to Kellogg, Aug. 27, 1839, Brown Collection, LC; Brown to Kellogg, Oct.17, 1842, Sanborn, *Life and Letters*, 55-56; Villard, *John Brown*, 30-31.
26. *Ibid.*, 31-33; Sanborn, *Life and Letters*, 134-135; W. E. B. DuBois, *John Brown* (Philadelphia, 1909), 53-54; Octavius B. Frothingham, *Gerrit Smith* (New York, 1877), 100.
27. Sanborn, *Life and Letters*, 135; Oberlin Board of Trustees resolutions.
28. *Ibid.*, 43, Two family additions, Oliver Brown (March 9, 1839) and Peter Brown (Dec. 10, 1840); Villard, *John Brown*, 32-33.
29. Boyer, *Legend of John Brown*, 340, Brown began herding sheep for Oviatt in 1841; Partnership agreement for tannery, dated Jan. 3, 1842, in Boyd B. Stutler Collection, HL.
30. *Ibid.*, 340-341; Settlement registered in Richfield, Ohio, Sept. 28, 1842, by George B. De Peyster, Stutler Collection, HL; Villard, *John Brown*, 42-43.
31. John Brown to John Brown, Jr., Jan. 11, 1844, John Brown, Jr. Papers, OHS; Boyer, *Legend of John Brown*, 339.
32. Villard, *John Brown*, 33-34; Sanborn, *Life and Letters*, 43.
33. John Brown to John Brown, Jr., Jan. 11, 1844, John Brown, Jr. Papers, OHS.
34. *Ibid.*, 57; *Ohio Cultivator*, Columbus, Aug. 15, 1845 cited by Boyer, *Legend of John Brown*, 347-48.

35. John Brown to John, Jr., March 24, 1845, John Brown, Jr., Papers, OHS; Perkins & Brown circular, written by Brown; E. C. Leonard anecdote, Sanborn, *Life and Letters*, 62-65; Villard, *John Brown*, 57; Oates, *To Purge This Land*, 54.

36. There are several studies of John Brown, the wool merchant. The best documented references are in Richard Boyer and Oswald G. Villard's biography. Stephen B. Oates and Robert Penn Warren leave both accurate and amusing accounts. All are cited above.

37. Brown to Perkins, Oct. ___, 1846, Perkins & Brown Letterbooks, 1846-1847, Stutler Collection, HL; Oates, *To Purge This Land*, 56.

38. *Ibid.*, 56-57; Erickson to Henry A. Wise, Nov. 8, 1859, John Brown Papers, LC; Villard, *John Brown*, 60-61.

39. *Ibid.*, 35-36; Brown to his wife, Nov. 8, 1846. Amelia was born June 22, 1845, and died Oct. 30, 1846.

40. *Ibid.*, 59-60; Brown to his father, Oct. 29, 1846, Sanborn, *Life and Letters*, 21; Oates, *To Purge This Land*, 56-57.

41. *Ibid.*, 62; Frederick Douglass, *Life and Times of....*(Hartford, CN, 1882), 277-280; Villard, *John Brown*, 57-58.

42. Boyer, *Legend of John Brown*, 368-374; Douglass, *Life and Times*, 280-282.

43. *Ibid.*, 44; Sanborn, *Life and Letters*, 96-97; Boyer, *Legend of John Brown*, 390-392.

Chapter Two

1. Frothingham, *Gerrit Smith*, 102-107, 235; Ralph V. Harlow, *Gerrit Smith, Philanthropist and Reformer* (New York, 939), 245-246; Sanborn, *Life and Letters*, 96-97.

2. *Ibid.*, 97; Redpath, *Public Life*, 59.

3. Boyer, *Legend of John Brown*, 392; Oates, *To Purge This Land*, 65.

4. *Ibid.*; Frothingham, *Gerrit Smith*, 234-235; Jeffery Rossbach, *Ambivalent Conspirators: John Brown, the Secret Six, and the Theory of Slave Violence* (Philadelphia, 1982), 92.

5. Frothingham, *Gerrit Smith*, 27-29.

6. Ralph V. Harlow, "Gerrit Smith and the Free Church Movement," *New York History*, 28 (July, 1937), 276; Ralph V. Harlow, *Gerrit Smith*, 16.

7. Frothingham, *Gerrit Smith*, 44-93, 98; John Brown Jr. to Sanborn, Nov. 11, 1887, Stutler Collection, HL; Boyer, *Legend of John Brown*, 325; Rossbach, *Ambivalent Conspirators*, 92-93.

8. Sanborn, *Life and Letters*, 40-41; Smith's humanity is covered in detail in Frothingham, *Gerrit Smith*, 94-143, and Harlow, *Gerrit Smith*, 200-390.

9. Louis Filler, ed., "John Brown in Ohio, An Interview with Charles F. F. Griffing," *Ohio State Archeological and Historical Quarterly*, Columbus, Ohio, April, 1849, 28; Boyer, *Legend of John Brown*, 215-216; Oates, *To Purge This Land*, 15, 42, 53, 58-59.

10. *Ibid.*, 58-59; Brown to John Jr., April 24, 1848, Villard Collection, CUL.

11. Frothingham, *Gerrit Smith*, 101; Thomas, John L., *The Liberator: William Lloyd Garrison* (Boston, 1963), 71-280; Oates, *To Purge This Land*, 28-29.

12. Lawrence W. Friedman, "The Gerrit Smith Circle: Abolitionism in the Burned-Over District," *Civil War History*, 26, (March, 1980), 23-24.

13. Frothingham, *Gerrit Smith*, 165-166.

14. *Ibid.*, 186-190; Rossbach, *Ambivalent Conspirators*, 94-95; Friedman, "Gerrit Smith Circle," 21-22.

15. Sanborn, *Life and Letters*, 98.

16. Donaldson, Alfred L., *A History of the Adirondacks*, 2 vols. (New York, 1921), II, 6.

17. Brown to his father, Jan. 10, 1849, Brown Papers, KSHS.

18. Sanborn, *Life and Letters*, 65-66; Boyer, *Legend of John Brown*, 394-395.

19. Villard, *John Brown*, 72-73.

20. Brown to Perkins, March 12, March 30, and May 24, 1849, John Brown Papers, LC; Boyer, *Legend of John Brown*, 395-396; Oates, *To Purge This Land*, 66-67.

21. Sanborn, *Life and Letters*, 67; Erikson to Wise, Nov. 8, 1859, John Brown Papers, LC; Boyer, *Legend of John Brown*, 380-381, 396-397.
22. Sanborn, *Life and Letters*, 99-100.
23. *Ibid.*, 100-101; Brown to Gerrit Smith, June 20, 1848, Stutler Collection, HL; Villard, *John Brown*, 72-73.
24. Boyer, *Legend of John Brown*, 406-407.
25. *Ibid.*, 407-413; Brown to John Brown Jr., Sept. 21, 1849, Sanborn, *Life and Letters*, 72-73; Brown to John Jr., Aug. 31, Sept. 21, and Oct. 5, 1849, John Brown Jr. Papers, OHS; Oates, *To Purge This Land*, 68-69.
26. *Ibid.*, 70-72; Brown to John Jr., Apr. 12, Nov. 4, Dec. 6 and Dec. 14, 1850, John Brown, Jr. Papers, OHS.
27. Frothingham, *Gerrit Smith*, 145, 210-212.
28. Brown to his wife, Nov. 28, 1850, Sanborn, *Life and Letters*, 106-107; Oates, *To Purge This Land*, 72.
29. Frothingham, *Gerrit Smith*, 209-210; Harlow, *Gerrit Smith*, 290-294; *The Liberator*, Aug. 16, 30, 1850; *The National Era*, Aug. 15, Sept. 15, 1850. Alexander Stephens later became the first and only vice president of the Confederacy.
30. Samuel J. May, *Some Recollections of our Anti-Slavery Conflict* (Boston, 1869), 373-83; Harlow, *Gerrit Smith*, 297-303.
31. *Ibid.*, 298; Warren, *John Brown*, 80. In 1851, Daniel Webster became Secretary of State.
32. Frothingham, *Gerrit Smith*, 118-119, 121.
33. Sanborn, *Life and Letters*, 123-124; Brown to wife, Jan. 17, 1851, ibid., 132; Villard, *John Brown*, 50-53; Oates, *To Purge This Land*, 72-73. Brown refers to Judges, 7, and Deuteronomy, 20.
34. Richard J. Hinton, *John Brown and His Men* (New York, 1894), 585-588, excerpt in Sanborn, *Life and Letters*, 132-133.
35. Sambo's Mistakes is printed in its entirety in Villard, *John Brown*, 659-661; and Sanborn, *Life and Letters*, 128-131.
36. *Ibid.*
37. Brown to family, Feb. 13, 1855, *ibid.*, 192; Boyer, *Legend of John Brown*, 457-458; Villard, *John Brown*, 75-76.
38. Frothingham, *Gerrit Smith*, 220-221.
39. *Ibid.*, 224.

Chapter Three

1. Frothingham, *Gerrit Smith*, 226.
2. Patricia L. Faust, ed., *Historical Times Illustrated: Encylopedia of the Civil War* (New York, 1986), 408.
3. Sanborn, *Life and Letters*, 188-189.
4. *Ibid.*, 191; Oates, *To Purge This Land*, 85.
5. Brown to Ruth and Henry Thompson, April 6 and June 10, 1853; Brown to family, Nov. 2, 1854, Sanborn, *Life and Letters*, 109, 110-111; Boyer, *Legend of John Brown*, 456-461.
6. Brown to family, June 4, 1855, Sanborn, *Life and Letters*, 193; also in Byron Reed Collection, OPL; Villard, *John Brown*, 75-76.
7. Sanborn, *Life and Letters*, 188-191, 194-198; John Jr. to John Sr., May 6, 1855, Sanborn-Brown Collection, HLHU.
8. Letter of John Brown dated May 20, 24 and 26, 1855, Dreer Collection, PHS in Villard, *John Brown*, 83-84; Jason Brown account, Dec. 13 and 14, 1908, Villard Collection, CU; Oates, *To Purge This Land*, 90.
9. *Ibid.*, 89; Sanborn, *Life and Letters*, 191, 197; Villard, *John Brown*, 81-82.

10. Brown to family, June 28, 1855, Sanborn, *Life and Letters*, 193-194; Harlow, *Gerrit Smith*, 339-341; Hinton, *John Brown*, 18-19; Boyer, *Legend of John Brown*, 526-527.

11. Frothingham, *Gerrit Smith*, 230-231.

12. Harlow, *Gerrit Smith*, 343-344; Sanborn, *Life and Letters*, 217-221; Villard, *John Brown*, 112-121 passim.

13. Harlow, *Gerrit Smith*, 345; Smith to Lawrence, Jan. 25, Feb. 3, 1856, Lawrence Letters, MHS, Vol. XIII, pp. 1511, 162; Lawrence to Smith, Jan. 29, 1856, Smith Papers, SUL.

14. Smith to Lasselle, Aug. 23, 1855, Smith Papers, USL.

15. Frothingham, *Gerrit Smith*, 232; Harlow, *Gerrit Smith*, 346-348. A complete copy of the speech is in the New York Public Library.

16. Financial report of New York State Kansas Aid Committee, Feb. 15 to July 10, 1856, Barnes Papers, KSHS; Smith to R. B. Miller, Smith Papers, SUL; Harlow, *Gerrit Smith*, 348-349.

17. Report of Buffalo meeting, June 9, 21, 26, 1856, Hyatt Papers and copy of Smith's speech, KSHS; Harlow, *Gerrit Smith*, 350-352.

18. *Ibid.*, 352-353.

19. Smith to Giddings, July 28, 1856, Giddings Papers, OHS.

20. Brown to family, Sanborn, *Life and Letters*, 199-200; Villard, *John Brown*, 85-86; Oates, *To Purge This Land*, 92-93; Warren, *John Brown*, 106.

21. Villard, *John Brown*, 95; In February, 1855, there were only 343 blacks in Kansas and of those, 151 were free negroes.

22. *Ibid.*, 98-99.

23. *Ibid.*, 97-98, 188; Charles Robinson, *Kansas Conflict* (Lawrence, 1898), 123-124; Sanborn, *Life and Letters*, 212.

24. Oates, *To Purge This Land*, 98-99, 101-103; Villard, *John Brown*, 105-106.

25. *Ibid.*, 112-116; John Brown Papers, KSHS (multiple documents); Sanborn, *Life and Letters*, 217-21.

26. *Ibid.*, 171-332; Villard, *John Brown*, 148-188; Oates, *To Purge This Land*, 97-137; Hinton, *John Brown*, 45-120, passim.

27. Villard, *John Brown*, 189-212; Oates, *To Purge This Land*, 152-154; Sanborn, *Life and Letters*, 244-303; Franklin B. Sanborn, *Recollections of Seventy Years* (Boston, 1909) 2 vols, I, 130-132; Warren, *John Brown*, 183-190.

28. Horace White Report, Sanborn, *Life and Letters*, 352-353; James Redpath reported $250,000 collected, which cannot be supported.

29. Sanborn, *Recollections*, I, 93-95; John Brown to Jason Brown, Aug. 11, 1856, Brown Papers, UK; John Brown, Jr. to John Brown, Aug. 16, 1856, Brown Papers, KSHS; Harlow, *Gerrit Smith*, 352-353; Villard, *John Brown*, 220-228; Oates, *To Purge This Land*, 160-162; James Malin, *John Brown and the Legend of Fifty-Six* (Philadelphia, 1942), 124-125, 606-609. Malin referred to John Brown as an insignificant frontier crook, a compulsive liar, a petty horse thief and a fraud.

30. For the Battle of Osawatomie, see Villard, *John Brown*, 239-246; Brown's Report, Sept. 7, 1856, and Luke Parson's statement, Sanborn, *Life and Letters*, 318-320, 285.

31. Robinson to Brown, Sanborn, *Life and Letters*, 330-331.

32. *Ibid.*, 342-343.

33. Webster to White, Oct. 25, 1856, Sanborn, *Life and Letters*, 341.

34. Watson Brown to family, Oct. 30, 1856, Brown Papers, KSHS; Villard, *John Brown*, 269-270. Salmon went on to Kansas, but was told erroneously that White had been killed. After that, he went back home. Watson stayed with his father.

35. *Ibid.*, 269; White to Brown, Oct. 26, 1856, Sanborn, *Life and Letters*, 342.

36. Chase Endorsement, December 20, 1856, *ibid.*, 363.

37. Villard, *John Brown*, 271 footnote.

Chapter Four

1. Smith to Brown, Dec. 30, 1856, Sanborn, *Life and Letters*, 364.
2. Sanborn, *Recollections*, I: 13-68; II: 261-328 passim; Rossbach, *Conspirators*, 46-54.
3. Henry Steele Commanger, *Theodore Parker, Yankee Crusader* (Boston, 1960), 7-222 passim.
4. As a general reference, see Samuel Gridley Howe, *The Letters and Journals of Samuel Gridley Howe*, Laura Richards, ed. (Boston, 1906), and Harold Schwartz, *Samuel Gridley Howe, Social Reformer* (Cambridge, 1952); Harlow, *Gerrit Smith*, 351; Rossbach, *Conspirators*, 26-30.
5. Frank Preston Stearns, *The Life and Public Services of George Luther Stearns* (Philadelphia, 1907), 13-130 passim; Howe, *Journals*, 417-419; Schwartz, *Howe*, 197-210, 205-206. Villard, *John Brown*, 272; Sanborn, *Recollections*, 51-52; Rossbach, *Conspirators*, 54-63.
6. Howard N. Meyer, *Colonel of the Black Regiment: The Life of Thomas Wentworth Higginson* (New York, 1967), 40-48; Tilden G. Edelstein, *Strange Enthusiasm: A Life of Thomas Wentworth Higginson* (New York, 1970), 7-52 passim, 56, 66-68.
7. *Ibid.*, 68-131 passim; Meyer, *Higginson*, 69-89 passim; Rossbach, *Conspirators*, 22-26.
8. National Kansas Committee resolutions, Jan. 24, and Horace White to Brown, Jan. 27, Feb. 18, Mar. 21, 1857, Sanborn, *Life and Letters*, 359-362; Stearns, *Stearns*, 129; Warren, *John Brown*, 227-231; Villard, *John Brown*, 274-276.
9. Subscriptions paid, Sanborn, *Life and Letters*, 111-114; Lawrence to Brown, Mar. 20, 1857, Brown Papers, MHS; Lawrence to Smith, Apr. 30, 1857, KSHS; Oates, *To Purge This Land*, 192-193.
10. Brown's speech to the Massachusetts Legislature, Feb. 18, 1857, Stutler Collection, HL; Villard, *John Brown*, 277-278; Sanborn, *Life and Letters*, 372-373.
11. *Ibid.*, 372-373, 387; Villard, *John Brown*, 277-278.
12. *Ibid.*, 282-283.
13. *Ibid.*, 283-285; Blair's testimony, *Report on the Invasion of Harpers Ferry*, U. S. Senate. Mason Committee. 36th Congress, 1st Session, 1860, Report. 278, I, 121-129.
14. Villard, *John Brown*, 285-287; Sanborn, *Life and Letters*, 388-390, 425-426; Harlow, *Gerrit Smith*, 394; Hinton, *John Brown*, 146-147; Oates, *To Purge This Land*, 200-201.
15. *Ibid.*, 200-205; Brown to John Jr., April 14, 1857, Stutler Collection, HL; Sanborn, *Life and Letters*, 509-511; Stearns' testimony, Mason Report, II, 227-228; Stearns, *Stearns*, 159; Villard, *John Brown*, 291-293.
16. *Ibid.*, 290-292; Brown to family, June 22, 1857, Stutler Collection, HL; Brown to family, June 25, 1857, ISHL; Smith to Hyatt, July 25, 1857, Hyatt Papers, KSHS; Brown to Stearns, Aug. 8, 1857, Sanborn, *Life and Letters*, 411-412; Harlow, *Gerrit Smith*, 394; Oates, *To Purge This Land*, 207.
17. *Ibid.*, 211-213; Forbes to Howe, May 14, 1858, *New York Herald*, Oct. 27, 1859; Villard, *John Brown*, 297-298; Harlow, *Gerrit Smith*, 394; Brown to Sanborn, Aug. 13, 1857, Sanborn, *Life and Letters*, 412-413, 399.
18. *Ibid.*, 397-398; Sanborn to Brown, Sept. 14, 19, and Oct. 19, 1857, Sanborn Papers, AUL; Brown to Higginson, Sept. 11, 1857, Higginson Papers, HLHU; Brown to Whitman, Oct. 5, 1857, Brown Papers, KSHS; Stearns to Whitman, Nov. 14, 1857, Stearns Papers, KSHS; Villard, *John Brown*, 303-305; Oates, *To Purge This Land*, 214-217.
19. *Ibid.*, 217-218; Stearns to Brown, Feb. 4, 1858, Stutler Collection, HL; Lane to Brown, Oct. 30, 1857, and Brown to Whitman, Oct. 24, 1857, Brown Papers, KSHS; Sanborn, *Life and Letters*, 425-430; Villard, *John Brown*, 298-299.
20. *Ibid.*, 317; Douglass, *Life and Times*, 317; Sanborn, *Life and Letters*, 433.
21. Douglass, *Life and Times*, 273-274; Provisional Constitution in Hinton, *John Brown*, 619-634.
22. Douglass, *Life and Times*, 317.

23. Brown to Higginson, Feb. 2, 1858, Higginson Papers, BPL; Brown to Parker, Feb. 2, 1858, Sanborn, *Life and Letters*, 434-436, 437; Sanborn, *Recollections*, I, 142-143; Oates, *To Purge This Land*, 225-227; Villard, *John Brown*, 320.

24. Harlow, *Gerrit Smith*, 396-397. Smith diary quoted in Frothingham, *Gerrit Smith*, 237.

25. Sanborn, *Recollections*, I, 144-145, 147-151; Sanborn, *Life and Letters*, 438-439; Villard, *John Brown*, 320-321; Harlow, *Gerrit Smith*, 397.

26. Sanborn, *Life and Letters*, 439.

27. *Ibid.*, 438-440; Smith to Lawrence, Feb. 25, 1856, Lawrence Collection, MHS; Harlow, *Gerrit Smith*, 345, 397; Sanborn, *Recollections*, I, 147.

28. Sanborn, *Life and Letters*, 439-440; Villard, *John Brown*, 321-322.

29. *Ibid.*, 320-321; Sanborn, *Life and Letters*, 442-443; Brown Diary, March 6,7, 1858, BPL; Thomas Wentworth Higginson, *Cheerful Yesterdays* (Boston, 1896), 219; Stearns, *Stearns*, 164.

30. Sanborn, *Life and Letters*, 445-448; Villard, *John Brown*, 324-326.

31. Smith to Giddings, Mar. 25, 1858 in Harlow, *Gerrit Smith*, 399.

32. Brown diary, Apr. 14, 1858, BPL; Sanborn to Higginson, May, 5, 1858, Higginson Collection, BPL; Brown to family, May 12, and Brown to Sanborn, May 14, 1858, Sanborn, *Life and Letters*, 455-457; Oates, *To Purge This Land*, 243-247; Villard, *John Brown*, 327-337.

33. Smith to Higginson, May 7, 1858, Higginson-Smith Collection, BPL; Sanborn, *Life and Letters*, 458.

34. *Ibid.*, 459; Higginson to Parker, May 9, 1858, Higginson-Parker Collection, BPL.

35. Stearns to Brown, May 14, 1858, Sanborn, *Life and Letters*, 461.

36. *Ibid.*, 463-464; Resolutions of the committee meeting are in the Higginson-Brown Collection, May __, 1858, BPL; Harlow, *Gerrit Smith*, 410-412; Villard, *John Brown*, 338-341.

37. Beckwith to Smith, May 27, 1858, Smith Papers, BPL; Harlow, *Gerrit Smith*, 401.

38. Smith to Sanborn, July 26, 1858, in Sanborn, *Recollections*, I, 160-161.

39. Villard, *John Brown*, 367-371.

40. Smith to wife, Jan. 10, 1859, Smith Papers, BPL; Harlow, *Gerrit Smith*, 403.

41. Brown's three month exodus out of Kansas is fully covered by Villard, *John Brown*, 369-390; Sanborn, *Life and Letters*, 469-494.

42. *Ibid.*, 492-493; Sanborn to Higginson, Mar. 4, 1859, Higginson Papers, BPL; Harlow, *Gerrit Smith*, 403.

Chapter Five

1. Frothingham, *Gerrit Smith*, 237. Anderson served Brown in Kansas and was acting as his bodyguard. He later died of bayonet wounds at Harpers Ferry.

2. Morton to Sanborn, April 13, 1859, Sanborn, *Life and Letters*, 467.

3. Sanborn, *Recollections*, I, 161-162; Villard, *John Brown*, 395; Harlow, *Gerrit Smith*, 403-404.

4. John Brown's diary, May 2, 1859, vol. 2, BPL.

5. Sanborn, *Life and Letters*, 467.

6. Morton to Sanborn, Apr. 13, June 30, 1859, *ibid.*, 467-68; Smith to Brown, June 4, 1859, *ibid.*, 524; Sanborn, *Recollections*, I, 165-166.

7. Sanborn, *Life and Letters*, 523; Sanborn to Higginson, May 30 and June 4, 1859, Higginson Papers, BPL; Higginson, *Cheerful Yesterdays*, 222-223; Schwartz, *Howe*, 239-240; Villard, *John Brown*, 396-397.

8. *Ibid.*, 402-408; Sanborn, *Life and Letters*, 527-529.

9. *Ibid.*, 544; Smith to John Thomas, Aug. 27, 1859, Smith Papers, SUL; Harlow, *Gerrit Smith*, 405-406.

10. *Ibid.*, 406-407; "A Southern Man" to Smith, Sept. 1859, Smith Papers, SUL.
11. Anonymous Letter to Floyd, Aug. 20, 1859, Sanborn, *Life and Letters*, 543; Villard, *John Brown*, 410-411; Frothingham, *Gerrit Smith*, 241.
12. Brown, Jr. to Kagi, Aug. 11, 1859, Mason Report, 68.
13. Brown to John Jr., Aug.___, 1859, Sanborn, *Life and Letters*, 535-536.
14. Sanborn to Brown, Aug. 30, 1859, *ibid.*, 535.
15. Oates, *To Purge This Land*, 284-285. For a biography of each of Brown's men, see Villard, *John Brown*, 678-687. For Brown's neighbors, see *ibid.* 403-425.
16. Sanborn, *Life and Letters*, 552-554; Villard, *John Brown*, 426-433; O. P. Anderson, *A Voice From Harpers Ferry* (Boston, 1861), 32-34; Hinton, *John Brown*, 708-709.
17. Daniel Whelan testimony in Mason Report, I: 22; Villard, *John Brown*, 430.
18. The raid on Harpers Ferry is covered in more than one hundred sources. The best documented accounts continue to be Villard, *John Brown*, 426-466, and Oates, *To Purge This Land*, 290-306.
19. "Black Republicans" is a generic term applied by Democrats to their Republican opponents and had nothing to do with skin color.
20. *New York Herald*, October 21, 1859; Sanborn, *Life and Letters*, 562-569; Villard, *John Brown*, 456-463.
21. Smith's letter to John Thomas, Chairman of Jerry Rescue Committee, Aug. 27, 1859, Smith Collection, SUL.
22. Harlow, *Gerrit Smith*, 441. Smith did not join the Republican Party until 1864.
23. *Ibid.*, 407; *New York Herald*, Oct. 20, 21, 1859; Villard, *John Brown*, 467; Oates, *To Purge This Land*, 301.
24. Douglass, *Life and Times*, 310-317, 325-330; Sanborn, *Recollections*, I, 187-207; Higginson, *Cheerful Yesterdays*, 223; Edelstein, *Strange Enthusiasm*, 221-232; Harlow, *Gerrit Smith*, 407-408.
25. *Ibid.*, 408; Sanborn, *Recollections*, I, 151n, 168-169. John Brown Jr. testimony, July 19, 1867, Brown Papers, KSHS.
26. Sterling to Smith, Oct. 21, 1859, Smith Papers, SUL.
27. Gibbs to Smith, Oct. 27, 1859, Smith Papers, SUL.
28. W. H. Fish to Smith, Oct. 25, 1859, Smith Papers, SUL; Harlow, *Gerrit Smith*, 408-409.
29. McCall to Smith, Oct. 28, 1859, Smith Papers, SUL.
30. "Gerrit Smith and the Harpers Ferry Outbreak," dated Peterboro, Oct. 31, 1859, in Harlow, *Gerrit Smith*, 410.
31. *Ibid.*; Frothingham, *Gerrit Smith*, 243.
32. Harlow, *Gerrit Smith*, 410-411.
33. *New York Herald*, Oct. 29, 1859.
34. Governor Wise speech, Oct. 21, 1859, in Villard, *John Brown*, 456.
35. Col. William Fellows in the *New York Sun*, Feb. 13, 1898, in Villard, *John Brown*, 554.
36. Sanborn, *Life and Letters*, 620; Villard, *John Brown*, 554.
37. *Ibid.*; *New York Herald*, Nov. 12, 1859.
38. Harlow, *Gerrit Smith*, 411.

Chapter Six

1. Redpath, *Public Life*, 403-405; Truman Nelson, *The Old Man: John Brown at Harpers Ferry* (New York, 1973), 279-280.
2. *New York Herald*, Dec. 8, 1859; Villard, *John Brown*, 561.
3. *A Tribute of Respect Commemorative of the Worth and Sacrifice of John Brown of Osawatomie: It Being a Full Report of the Speeches Made and the Resolutions Adopted by the Citizens of Cleveland* [Dec. 2, 1859]...(Cleveland, 1859), in Oates, *To Purge This Land*, 354.

4. Dr. Gray to John Cochrane, Dec. 15, 1859, Smith Papers, SUL; Harlow, *Gerrit Smith*, 409, 412-413; Frothingham, *Gerrit Smith*, 245-246.

5. Cochrane to Smith, Mar. 17, draft of Smith's reply, Mar. 21, and Dr. Gray to Miller, Apr. 9, 1860, Smith Letters, SUL. Committee consisted of James M. Mason, Chairman, Jefferson Davis, G. N. Fitch, Jacob Collamer, and James R. Doolittle. Mason Report, I, 29-30, 38; for Stearns' and Howe's testimony, see 225-251, 157-178; Rossbach, *Conspirators*, 236-266; Harlow, *Gerrit Smith*, 413-414.

6. Smith to Sumner, June 7, 1860, and Cochrane to Smith, June 19, 1860, Smith Papers, SUL.

7. Harlow, *Gerrit Smith*, 415-416; Miller to Sherman, Feb. 13, Barlow to Miller, Feb. 22, and Miller to Barlow, Feb. 26, 1860, Smith Letters, SUL; *Syracuse Journal*, Feb. 29, 1869; Frothingham, *Gerrit Smith*, 251-252.

8. *Ibid.*, 452-459; Ralph V. Harlow, "Gerrit Smith and the John Brown Raid." *American Historical Review*, 38 (October, 1932), 57; Harlow, *Gerrit Smith*, 416-417.

9. *Ibid.*, 417-419; Spooner to Smith, Aug. 29, 1860, Smith Papers, SUL; Villard, *John Brown*, 514.

10. Smith to Spooner, Oct. 25, 1860, Smith Papers, SUL; Harlow, *Gerrit Smith*, 419-420; Harlow, "Gerrit Smith and John Brown," 57-58.

11. *Chicago Tribune*, June 13, 1865; Frothingham, *Gerrit Smith*, 261; Harlow, *Gerrit Smith*, 451.

12. *Ibid.*, 450-451; *Chicago Tribune*, Nov. 25, Dec. 25, 1865; Smith to Farwell, Nov. 25, and Farwell to Smith, Dec. 26, 1865, Smith Papers, SUL; Harlow, "Gerrit Smith and John Brown," 58-59; Frothingham, *Gerrit Smith*, 261.

13. *Albany Argus*, Dec. 28, 1865 in Harlow, *Gerrit Smith*, 451.

14. Farwell to Smith, June 1, and Oct. 15, 1866, Smith Papers, SUL.

15. Farwell to Smith, Jan. 8, July 6, 9, and Sedgwick to Smith, July 1, 1867, Smith Papers, SUL; Harlow, *Gerrit Smith*, 452-453.

16. *Chicago Tribune*, July 22, 1867, Smith Papers, SUL; Harlow, *Gerrit Smith*, 453; Frothingham, *Gerrit Smith*, 261-262.

17. *Chicago Tribune*, July 29, 1867.

18. Harlow, *Gerrit Smith*, 453-454.

19. Gerrit Smith's "John Brown," Aug. 15, 1867, is printed in Frothingham, *Gerrit Smith*, (first ed.), 253-259.

20. White to Smith, Aug. 20, 1867 in Frothingham, *Gerrit Smith*, 264.

21. Corliss to Smith, Sept. 29, 1859, in Harlow, "Gerrit Smith and John Brown," 49.

22. *Ibid.*, 48; Smith to Sanborn, Oct. 19, 1872, in Franklin B. Sanborn, "A Concord Note-Book, Gerrit Smith and John Brown." *The Critic*, vol. 47, Oct., 1905, 353.

23. Frothingham, *Gerrit Smith*, 359-360; *New York Evening Mail*, Dec. 28, 1874.

24. *New York Times*, Dec. 29, 1874.

25. Sanborn, "A Concord Note-Book," 349.

Bibliography

MANUSCRIPTS AND DOCUMENTS

Atlanta University Library (AUL), Atlanta Georgia
    Brown (John) Papers in Brown-Thompson Papers located in the Slaughter Collection.
    Sanborn (Franklin B.) Papers.
Boston Public Library (BPL), Boston, MA.
    Brown (John) Diary.
    Higginson-Brown Collection.
    Higginson-Parker Collection.
    Higginson-Sanborn Collection.
    Higginson-Smith Collection.
Columbia University (CU), New York, NY.
    Villard (Oswald Garrison) Collection.
Houghton Library, Harvard University (HLHU), Cambridge, MA.
    Higginson (Thomas Wentworth) Collection.
    Sanborn-Brown Collection.
    Smith (Gerrit) Collection.
    Stearns (George Luther) Collection.
Huntington Library (HL), Charleston, West Virginia.
    Brown Family Papers, Boyd B. Stutler Collection.
Illinois State Historical Library (ISHL),Springfield, IL.
    Brown (John) Papers.
Kansas State Historical Society (KSHS), Topeka, KS.
    Barnes (Gilbert) Papers.
    Brown Family Papers.
    Hyatt (Thaddeus) Papers.
    Lawrence (Amos A.) Papers.
    Sanborn (Franklin B.) Papers.
    Smith (Gerrit) Papers.
    Stearns (George Luther) Collection.
Library of Congress (LC), Washington, DC.
    Brown Family Collection.
Massachusetts Historical Society (MHS), Boston, MA.
    Brown Family Collection.
    Howe (Samuel Gridley) Papers.

Lawrence (Amos A.) Collection.
Stearns (George Luther) Collection.
New York Public Library (NYPL), New York, NY.
Smith (Gerrit) Collection.
Ohio Historical Society (OHS), Columbus, OH.
Brown (John) Papers.
Brown (John, Jr.) Papers.
Giddings (Joshua R.) Papers.
Omaha Public Library (OPL), Omaha, NE.
Reed (Byron) Collection.
Pennsylvania Historical Society (PHS), Philadelphia, PA.
Dreer (Ferdinand Julius) Papers.
Syracuse University Library (SUL), Syracuse, NY.
Smith (Gerrit) Collection.
University of Kansas (UK), Lawrence, KS.
Brown-Pate Kansas Collection.

NEWSPAPERS

Albany *Argus*
The Liberator
New York *Herald*
New York *Tribune*

Chicago *Tribune*
National Era
New York *Sun*
Ohio Cultivator

Kent *Courier*
New York *Evening Mail*
New York *Times*
Syracuse *Journal*

BOOKS, ARTICLES AND REPORTS

Abels, Jules. *Man on Fire-John Brown and the Cause of Liberty*. New York: The Macmillan Company, 1971.
Anderson, Osborne P. *A Voice From Harpers Ferry....* Boston: by the author, 1861.
Avey, Elijah. *The Capture and Execution of John Brown—A Tale of Martrydom*. Elgin, IL: Brethren Publishing House, 1943.
Barry, Joseph. *The Annals of Harpers Ferry*. Hagerstown: Dechert & Co., 1872.
Blight, David W. *Frederick Douglass' Civil War-Keeping Faith in Jubilee*. Baton Rouge: Louisiana State University, 1989.
Boteler, Alexander R. "Recollections of the John Brown Raid." *Century Magazine*, July, 1883.
Boyer, Richard O. *The Legend of John Brown*. New York: Alfred A. Knopf, 1973.
Brewerton, G. D. *The War in Kansas*. New York: Derby and Jackson, 1856.
Brown, G. W. *Reminiscences of Old John Brown*. Rockford, IL: Abraham E. Smith, 1880.
Brown, Salmon. "My Father, John Brown." *Outlook*, January 25, 1913.
Buley, R. Carlyle. *The Old Northwest: Pioneer Period, 1815-1840*. 2 vols. Bloomington, IN: Indiana University, 1951.
Bushong, Millard K. *Historic Jefferson County*. Boyce, VA: Carr Publishing Company, Inc., 1972.
Chamberlain, Joseph Edgar. *John Brown*. Boston: Small, Maynard and Co., 1899.
Commanger, Henry Steele. *Theodore Parker*. Boston: Little, Brown, and Company, 1936.
Connolley, William E. *John Brown*. Topeka, Kansas: Crane & Co., 1900.
Daingerfield, John E. P. "John Brown At Harpers Ferry." *Century Magazine*, June, 1885.
Donaldson, Alfred L. *A History of the Adirondacks*. New York: Putnam's Sons, 1921.
Douglass, Frederick. *The Life and Times of....* London: Christian Age Office, 1884.
Doy, John. *Narrative of John Doy of Lawrence, Kansas*. New York: Thomas Halman, 1860.
Du Bois, W. E. Burghardt. *John Brown*. Philadelphia: George W. Jacobs & Co., 1909.

Edelstein, Tilden G. *Strange Enthusiasm: A Life of Thomas Wentworth Higginson*. New York: Atheneum, 1970.

Ehrlich, Leonard. *God's Angry Man*. New York: Simon and Schuster, Inc., 1932.

Faust, Patricia L., ed. *Historical Times Illustrated: Encyclopedia of the Civil War*. New York: Harper and Row, 1986.

Filler, Louis, ed. "John Brown in Ohio, An Interview with Charles F. F. Griffing." *Ohio State Archeological and Historical Quarterly*, Columbus, OH, April, 1849.

Franklin, John H. *From Slavery to Freedom*. New York: Alfred A. Knopf, 1947.

Friedman, Lawrence J. "The Gerrit Smith Circle: Abolitionism in the Burned-Over District." *Civil War History*, 26 (March, 1980): 18-38.

Frothingham, Octavius Brooks. *Gerrit Smith: A Biography*. New York: G. P. Putnam's Sons, 1878.

————. *Theodore Parker: A Biography*. Boston: James R. Osgood and Co., 1874.

Furnas, J. C. *The Road to Harpers Ferry*. New York: William Sloane Associates, 1959.

Green, Israel. "The Capture of John Brown." *North American Review*, December, 1855.

Greene, Laurence. *The Raid—A Biography of Harpers Ferry*. New York: Henry Holt and Co., 1953.

Hamilton, James Cleland. "John Brown in Canada." *Canadian Magazine*, December, 1894.

Harlow, Ralph Volney. *Gerrit Smith: Philanthropist and Reformer*. New York: Henry Holt & Co., 1939.

————. "Gerrit Smith and the John Brown Raid." *American Historical Review*, 38 (October, 1932): 35-57.

————. "Gerrit Smith and the Free Church Movement." *New York History*, 18 July, 1937.

Higginson, Mary Potter Thatcher. *Thomas Wentworth Higginson: The Story of His Life*. Boston: Houghton Mifflin Co., 1914.

Higginson, Thomas Wentworth. *Cheerful Yesterdays*. Boston: Houghton Mifflin Co., 1921.

Hinton, Richard J. *John Brown and His Men....* New York: Funk and Wagnalls, 1894.

————. *Rebel Invasion of Missouri and Kansas*. Chicago: Church and Goodman, 1865.

Howe, Julia Ward. *Memoir of Dr. Samuel Gridley Howe....* Boston: Howe Memorial Committee, 1876.

Howe, Samuel Gridley. *The Letters and Journals of....* Laura E. Richards, ed., 2 vols. Boston: Dana, Estes and Co., 1906.

Hungerford, Edward. *The Story of the Baltimore & Ohio Railroad*. 2 vols. New York: Putnam's Sons, 1928.

Karsner, David. *John Brown, Terrible Saint*. New York: Dodd, Mead and Company, 1934.

Keller, Allan. *Thunder At Harpers Ferry*. Englewood Cliffs, NJ: Prentice-Hall, Inc., 1958.

Land, Mary. "John Brown's Ohio Environment." *Ohio State Archaeological and Historical Quarterly*. January, 1948.

Malin, James C. *John Brown and the Legend of Fifty-Six*. Philadelphia: The American Philosophical Society, 1942.

May, Samuel J. *Some Recollections of Our Anti-Slavery Conflict*. Boston: Fields, Osgood & Co., 1869.

Meyer, Howard N. *Colonel of the Black Regiment-The Life of Thomas Wentworth Higginson*. New York: W. W. Norton and Co. Inc., 1967.

Nelson, Truman. *The Old Man–John Brown At Harpers Ferry*. New York: Holt, Rinehart, Winston, 1973.

Newton, John. *Captain John Brown of Harpers Ferry*. New York: A. Wessels Co., 1902.

Nichols, Alice. *Bleeding Kansas*. New York: Oxford University Press, 1954.

Oates, Stephen B. *To Purge This Land With Blood*. Amherst, MA: University of Massachusetts Press, 1970.

Orpen, Adela E. *Memories of Old Emigrant Days in Kansas*. New York: Harper & Brothers, 1928.

Pate, Henry Clay. *John Brown as Viewed by H. Clay Pate*. New York: by the author, 1859.

Phillips, William A. "Three Interviews with John Brown." *Atlantic Monthly*, December, 1879.

Potter, David M. *The Impending Crisis, 1848-1861*. New York: Harper & Row, 1976.

Redpath, James. *Echoes of Harpers Ferry*. Boston: Thayer and Eldridge, 1860.

_____. *The Public Life of Captain John Brown*.... Boston: Thayer and Eldridge, 1860.

Richards, Laura E. *Samuel Gridley Howe*. New York: D. Appleton-Century Co., 1935.

Richman, Irving B. *John Brown Among the Quakers*.... Des Moines: The Historical Department of Iowa, 1894.

Robinson, Charles. *The Kansas Conflict*. Lawrence, KS: Journal Publishing Co., 1898.

Rossbach, Jeffery. *Ambivalent Conspirators*. Philadelphia: University of Pennsylvania Press, 1982.

Rosengarten, John G. "John Brown's Raid: How I Got Into It, and How I Got Out of It." *Atlantic Monthly*, June, 1865.

Ruchames, Louis, ed. *A John Brown Reader*. New York: Abelard-Schuman, 1959.

Saddler, Harry Dean. *John Brown-The Magnificent Failure*. Philadelphia: Dorrance & Co., 1951.

Sanborn, Franklin B. *Dr. S. G. Howe, The Philanthropist*. New York: Funk and Wagnalls, 1891.

_____. *The Life and Letters of John Brown, Liberator of Kansas and Martyr of Virginia*. Boston: Roberts Bros., 1885.

_____. *Recollections of Seventy Years*. 2 vols. Boston: Richard G. Badger, 1909.

_____. "A Concord Note-Book, Gerrit Smith and John Brown." *The Critic*, vol. 47, Oct., 1905, 349-356.

Schwartz, Harold. *Samuel Gridley Howe: Social Reformer, 1801-1876*. Cambridge, MA: Harvard University Press, 1956.

Smith, Merritt Roe. *Harpers Ferry Armory and the New Technology*. Ithaca, NY: Cornell University Press, 1977.

Stavis, Barrie. *John Brown-The Sword and the Word*. New York: A. S. Barnes and Company, 1970.

Stearns, Frank Preston. *The Life and Public Services of George Luther Stearns*. Philadelphia: J.B. Lippincott Company, 1907.

_____. "John Brown and His Eastern Friends." *New England Magazine*, July, 1910.

Stutler, Boyd B. "The Hanging of John Brown." *American Heritage*, February, 1955.

_____. "John Brown and the Oberlin Lands." *West Virginia History*, April, 1951.

Thomas, John L. *The Liberator: William Lloyd Garrison*. Boston: Little, Brown Co., 1963.

United States Senate. Mason Committee. *Report on the Invasion of Harpers Ferry*. 36th Congress, 1st session, 1860, Report 278.

Utter, Davis N. "John Brown of Osawattomie." *North American Review*, November, 1883.

Villard, Oswald Garrison. *John Brown: 1800-1859-A Biography Fifty Years After*. [Revised Edition.] New York: Alfred A. Knopf, 1943.

War of the Rebellion—Official Records of the Union and Confederate Armies. 128 vols. Washington, DC: Government Printing Office, 1880-1901.

Warren, Robert Penn. *John Brown: The Making of a Martyr*. New York: Payson and Clarke, Ltd., 1929.

Wilson, Hill Peebles. *John Brown, Soldier of Fortune*. Boston: The Cornhill Co., 1918.

Wyatt-Brown, Bertram. *Yankee Saints and Southern Sinners*. Baton Rouge: Louisiana State University, 1985.

Index

Chester Hearn first became interested in the story of John Brown during his freshman year at Allegheny College in 1950. Later, he spent many years researching and collecting data on John Brown and developed a fascination with other key characters in the ill-fated Harpers Ferry raid. The result is *Companions in Conspiracy*, which focuses particularly on Gerrit Smith, a member of the Secret Six who secretly financed the raiders, and his strange and tangled relationship with John Brown.

Educated at Allegheny College in Meadville, Pennsylvania, Chester Hearn served in the U.S. Army from 1954-1956. He is the author of four other books on military history, including *Gray Raiders of the Sea, Mobile Bay and the Mobile Campaign*, and *The Capture of New Orleans, 1862*. He resides in Potts Grove, Pennsylvania, with his wife, Ann.